Presented to

_____

on

_____

by

_____

# My
# Bible

## God's Word
## for Me

Written by
**Mary Martha
Moss, FSP**

Illustrated by
**Augusta Curreli**

Pauline
BOOKS & MEDIA
Boston

*Imprimatur:* ✠ Most Reverend Gregory M. Aymond
Archbishop of New Orleans
December 13, 2018

Library of Congress Control Number: 2019937414
CIP data is available.

ISBN 0–8198-5004-7
ISBN 978–0-8198-5004-1

Cover design by Mary Joseph Peterson, FSP
Cover art and illustrations by Augusta Curreli
Maps by Chris Sabatino

Published by Pauline Books & Media, 50 Saint Pauls Avenue, Boston, MA 02130–3491

Printed in Korea

MBGWFM SIPSKOGUNKYO3-18071 5004-7

www.pauline.org

Pauline Books & Media is the publishing house of the Daughters of St. Paul, an international congregation of women religious serving the Church with the communications media.

1 2 3 4 5 6 7 8 9                                   23 22 21 20 19

*Dedicated to*

*Hayley Elizabeth Manning,*

*Kessler Gordon Brown,*

*and George Thomas Moss II.*

*May the Bible stories of God's love*

*always fill your heart with joy.*

# Contents

# Introduction

Throughout your life you will read many interesting books. Some books will teach you things. Other books will take you on imaginative adventures. And one book will show you God's amazing plan for the world—and for you! The Bible tells the incredible story of God's love for us.

God made everything, including human beings. Why? Because he wanted to share his love. He made us so that one day we will be with him in heaven. But God does not force us to love him. Instead, he gave us freedom. Sadly, with that freedom we've made some bad decisions. Adam and Eve hurt humanity by sinning.

But hope is not lost! The Bible is full of heroes and heroines who have made the right decisions! Many men and women believed in God's love for us and did brave and daring things to help others know God's care for the world. Noah listens to God and learns how to build an ark to save his family and animals from a great flood. God tells Moses to use his staff to heal snake bites and to part the Red Sea. And God sends an angel to ask Mary if she will be the mother of Jesus, who came to save us!

This amazing story of God's saving love is now part of each of our lives. Every time you read the Scriptures you meet God. Whether you read the stories in order or jump around, they each contain something important that God wants you to know. And in every story, we can hear God saying to each of us, over and over again: I love you!

# Old Testament

# Creation

In the beginning there was nothing—not one thing! Only God existed. God made everything in the world out of nothing.

First God said, "Let there be light," and then there was light! Then God made the sky, the sea, and the earth. God made all kinds of trees and plants. Next God made the sun, the moon, and the stars. God saw that it was good.

There were no living creatures in the waters yet, so God made dolphins, whales, and fish of every kind. God also made birds that fly in the sky. Then God made all sorts of land animals: cows, horses, kangaroos, and all the other wild and tame animals too. And God saw that it was good.

God loved everything he had created, but he was not yet finished. So God made the first man, Adam. God put Adam in charge of all creation, even the animals. Then God said, "Adam needs a helper, so he will not be alone." While Adam slept, God made the first woman. When Adam awoke, he was so happy. "There she is at last!" he exclaimed. He called the woman Eve. God looked at them and blessed them. And God saw that it was all very good.

These are the six days of creation. On the seventh day God finished his work and rested.

*You made everything good, O God.*
*Thank you for your gifts!*

# Adam and Eve in the Garden

*Genesis 3*

God loved Adam and Eve and placed them in a beautiful garden. In the garden everything was perfect. There was no illness or death or sadness. Every evening God walked with the man and the woman. God asked Adam and Eve to care for the garden and its creatures. God also

told them that they could eat fruit from all the trees except for one. They were not to eat fruit from the tree in the middle of the garden. "If you eat it," God said, "you will die."

Every day Adam and Eve talked to God and walked with him. They were very happy.

One day the serpent approached Eve. "Did God really tell you not to eat the fruit from this tree?" he asked.

"We can eat from every tree in the garden except this one," she answered. "If we eat its fruit, we will die!"

"That's not true," the serpent lied. "If you eat this fruit, you will know everything, just like God does. You will be like God!"

Eve chose to listen to the serpent and to disobey God. She took some of the fruit, ate it, and gave some to Adam. He also ate it. Adam and Eve both disobeyed God. At that moment they realized that they were not wearing any clothes.

When God came to visit them, they were ashamed and hid themselves. God already knew they had sinned by choosing not to listen to him. "You cannot live in this perfect garden anymore," God told them sadly.

God still loved Adam and Eve, so he made them a promise. God would one day send a Savior to save them from sin.

*God, may I always listen to your voice and do your will with love.*

# Cain and Abel

*Genesis 4*

Adam and Eve had two sons. Cain was a farmer. He grew vegetables and fruit. Abel was a shepherd. He took care of sheep.

One day both brothers offered a sacrifice of gifts to God. Because Abel loved God so much, he gave God the very best of his flock. Cain brought God some fruit, but not the best produce of his land. God knew what was in each brother's heart. God was pleased with Abel's gift, but not with Cain's.

Cain then grew angry and was jealous of his brother. God warned Cain, "If you give your best, it will be accepted. Control your temper so you do not sin."

Cain did not obey God. Instead he said to Abel, "Let us go out to the field."

When the brothers arrived, Cain killed Abel!

God knew what Cain had done. But God still asked Cain, "Where is Abel?"

Cain pretended he did not know. "Am I in charge of my brother's care?" he sneered.

After this terrible sin, God sent Cain away. Cain was worried that other people would hurt him. But God still loved Cain, so he promised to protect him from harm.

*Lord, may I always give you the best of what I have and what I am.*

# Noah and the Flood

*Genesis 6–9*

Adam and Eve had other children, grandchildren, and great-grandchildren. As the years passed, many people lived on the earth.

Over time more and more people disobeyed God and sinned. They did not want to follow God's way. Eventually, most people chose evil and the Earth became a violent place. Seeing this, God was sorry he had made humans.

One man and his family, however, were still obedient to God. The man's name was Noah, and he loved God very much. God told Noah that he was going to send a terrible flood. It would wash away all the evil in the world. God wanted to keep Noah and his family safe. So he told Noah to build an ark out of wood. Then he told Noah to fill the ark with two of every kind of creature that lived on the earth.

Noah believed God and did as God asked. When the ark was built, it was big enough for Noah, his family, and a male and female of every kind of animal.

Then the rain started. It rained for forty days and forty nights. Water covered the entire world! Only the creatures of the sea and the creatures on the ark lived. Noah, his family, and the animals were all safe as the ark floated on the water.

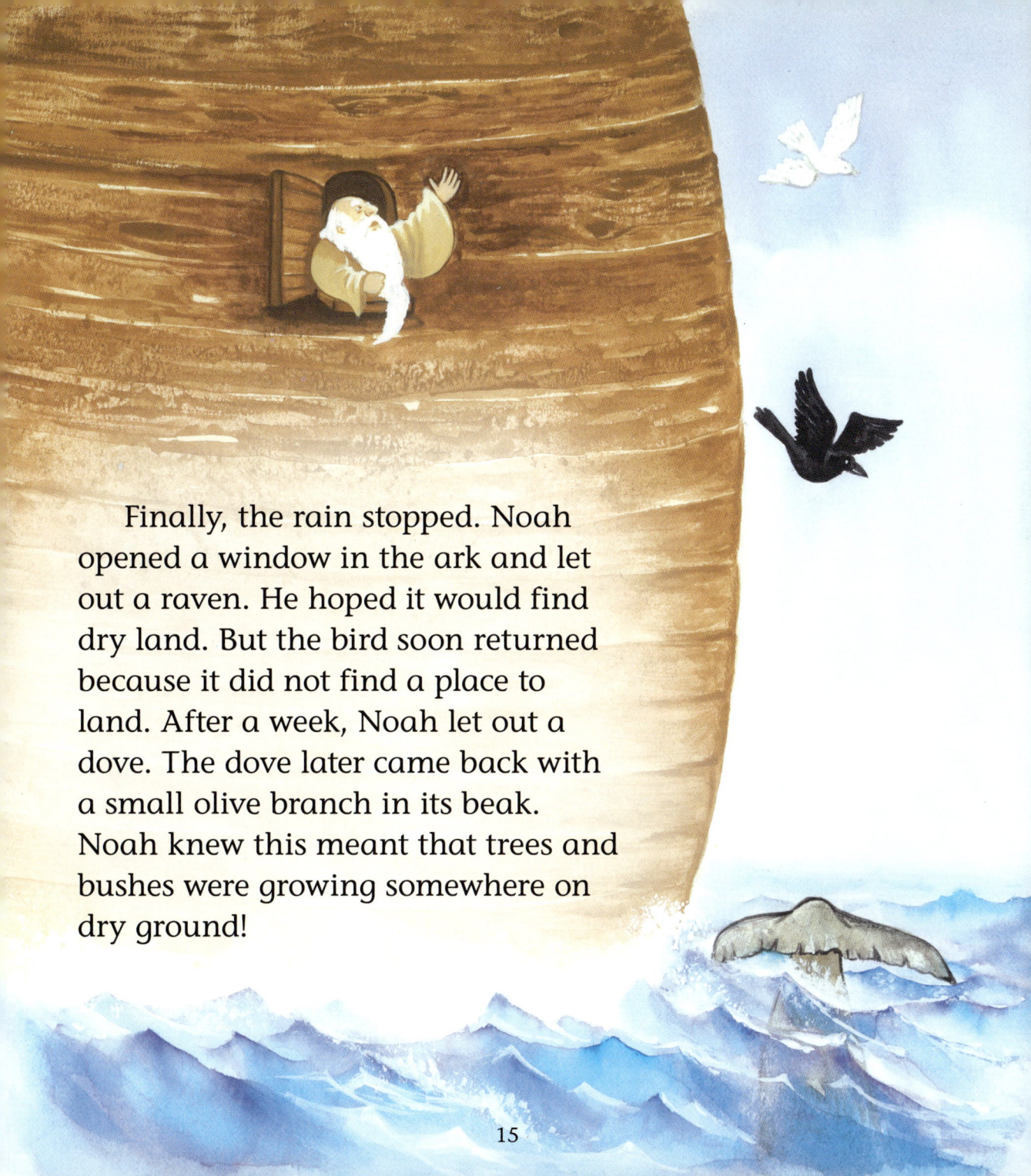

Finally, the rain stopped. Noah opened a window in the ark and let out a raven. He hoped it would find dry land. But the bird soon returned because it did not find a place to land. After a week, Noah let out a dove. The dove later came back with a small olive branch in its beak. Noah knew this meant that trees and bushes were growing somewhere on dry ground!

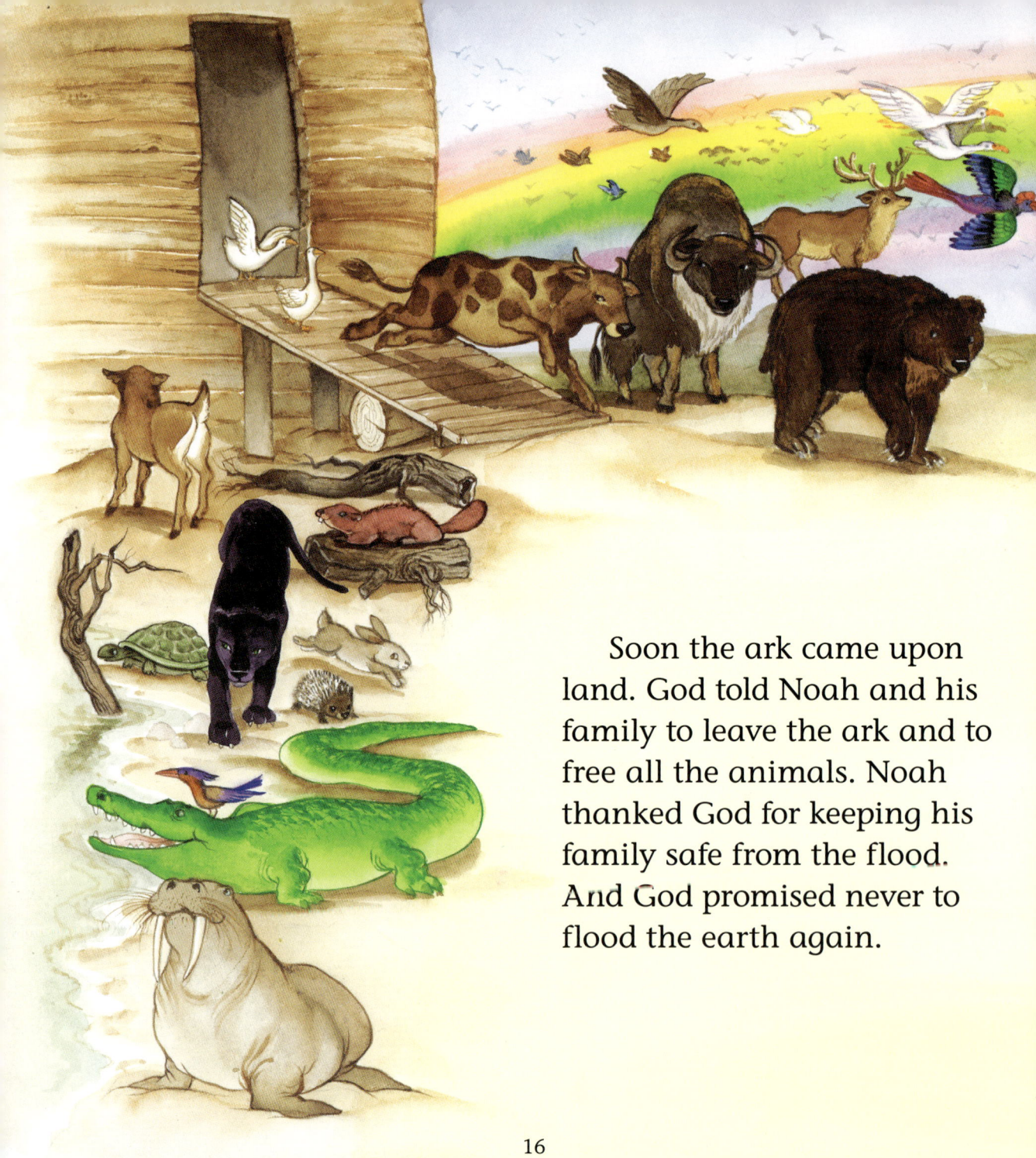

Soon the ark came upon land. God told Noah and his family to leave the ark and to free all the animals. Noah thanked God for keeping his family safe from the flood. And God promised never to flood the earth again.

God blessed Noah and his
family. Then God sent a beautiful
rainbow in the sky as the sign of
his promise, or *covenant*, never to
flood the earth again. "See," God
said, "I have put my rainbow in
the clouds to remind you of my
covenant with you and all living
things."

*O God, help me listen to you and
choose to do what is right.*

# God Calls Abram to Leave His Homeland

*Genesis 12*

In the land of Haran lived a good man named Abram. One day God told him, "I want you to leave this place and go to a land that I will show you. There I will bless you and make of you a great nation. Everyone after you will be blessed through you and your family."

Abram trusted God and did what God asked. Abram was seventy-five years old when he set out with his wife, Sarai, and his nephew Lot. They took with them all of their servants, their possessions, and their animals.

After many days of travel, at last they arrived in Canaan. There God told Abram, "I will give this land to your children." Abram was grateful to God. He built an altar and worshiped God there.

*O God, help me to know that you are always with me.*

19

# Melchizedek

*Genesis 14*

One day, Abram learned that his nephew Lot had been taken prisoner. Abram called his friends and went to rescue him. They tracked down the bad men and overpowered them. Abram then returned home with Lot and all that had been stolen from Lot's people.

When they arrived they met Melchizedek, who was both a priest and King of Salem. Melchizedek gave thanks to God. He offered bread and wine, saying, "May you be blessed, Abram, by God who made heaven and earth. Let us bless God who helped you defeat your enemies!"

*All true peace (salem) comes from you, O God. Thank you for helping me in times of need.*

# Abraham and Sarah

*Genesis 15, 17*

Abram remembered God's promise to make of him a great nation. But Abram and Sarai were childless, and both were very old. God told Abram, "Do not fear, Abram! I will bless you greatly." He took Abram outside, then God told Abram that his descendants would be like the stars—countless. And Abram put his faith in God.

Abram was now ninety-nine years old. He and Sarai still had no children. Then God said to him, "No longer will you be called Abram. Your name is now Abraham, for I will make you the father of many nations. Our covenant is everlasting. You and your descendants will be my people and I will be your God. Your wife's name is now Sarah. I will bless her with a baby boy."

Abraham laughed. Surely he and Sarah were too old to have a child!

But God kept his promise. He gave Abraham and Sarah a son named Isaac. They rejoiced that God was faithful to his covenant.

*Help me, O God, to always trust in your promises.*

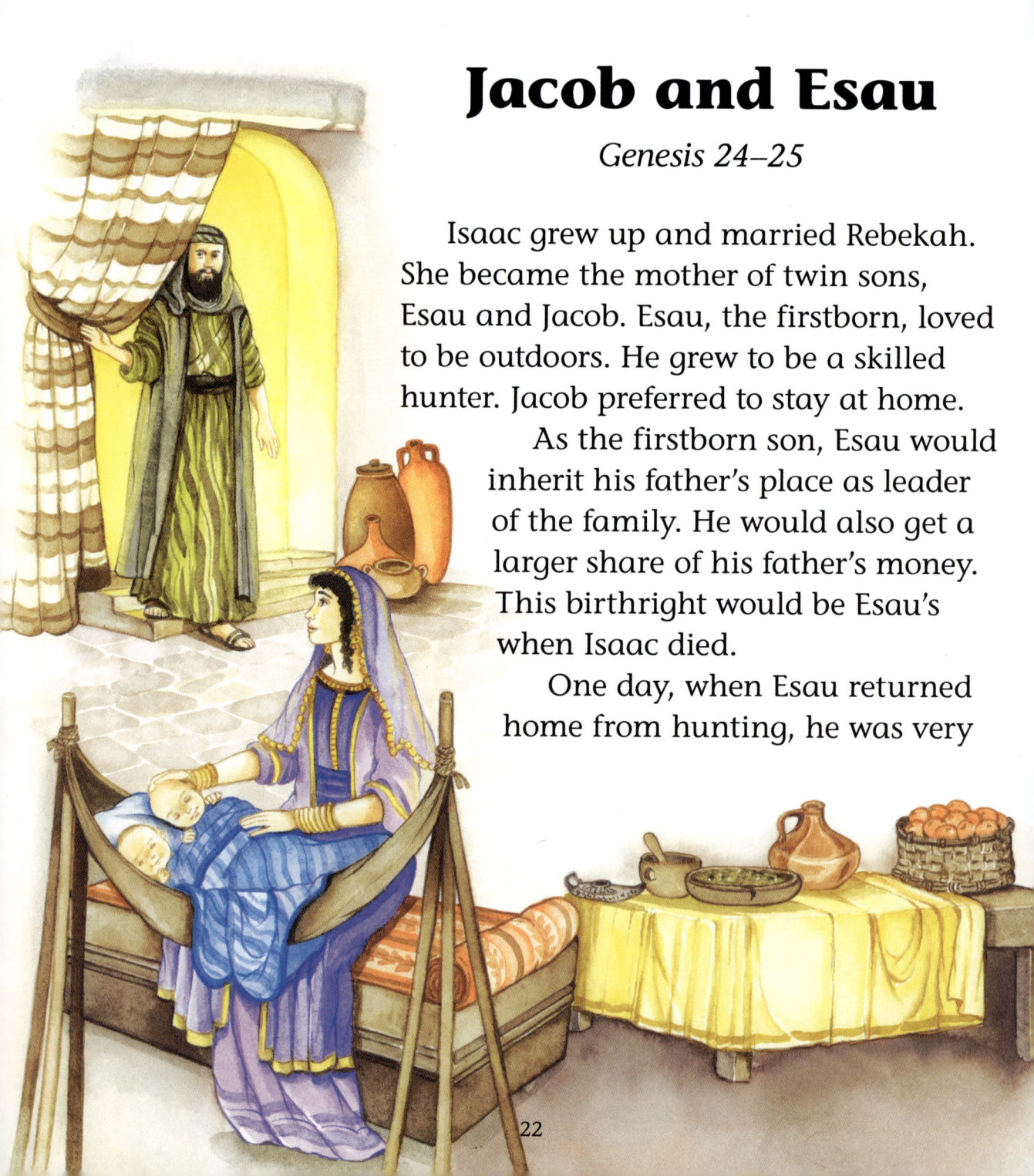

# Jacob and Esau

*Genesis 24–25*

Isaac grew up and married Rebekah. She became the mother of twin sons, Esau and Jacob. Esau, the firstborn, loved to be outdoors. He grew to be a skilled hunter. Jacob preferred to stay at home.

As the firstborn son, Esau would inherit his father's place as leader of the family. He would also get a larger share of his father's money. This birthright would be Esau's when Isaac died.

One day, when Esau returned home from hunting, he was very

hungry. He smelled the stew Jacob was cooking and demanded, "Give me some of that." Jacob knew how hungry Esau was and thought it was a good opportunity to get something from his brother. So Jacob said, "I will give you some if you give me your birthright." Esau replied, "I'm starving! What good is a birthright to me?" But Jacob made him promise. This was how Esau sold his birthright to Jacob.

*Lord, help me to recognize and be grateful for the gifts you give to me.*

23

# Isaac Blesses Jacob

*Genesis 27*

Many years later, when Isaac was very old, he could no longer see. Before he died he wanted to give his firstborn a special blessing. So he called for Esau and told him to hunt and prepare food for him. Then Isaac would bless him.

Esau left, but Rebekah had overheard everything. She favored Jacob over Esau. So Rebekah quickly called Jacob and presented a plan. She would prepare the meal, and Jacob would pretend to be Esau and

bring the food to Isaac. Jacob reminded her, "But I am not hairy like Esau. My father will know I am not him." So Rebekah covered Jacob's arms with goatskins. She also dressed him in Esau's clothes. Jacob then brought the food to his father. Isaac was fooled. He gave Esau's firstborn blessing to Jacob. Isaac said, "May you have the best things on the earth and from heaven. May your brother bow to you and all people honor you. May those who bless you be blessed themselves!"

*Lord, make me a blessing for others.*

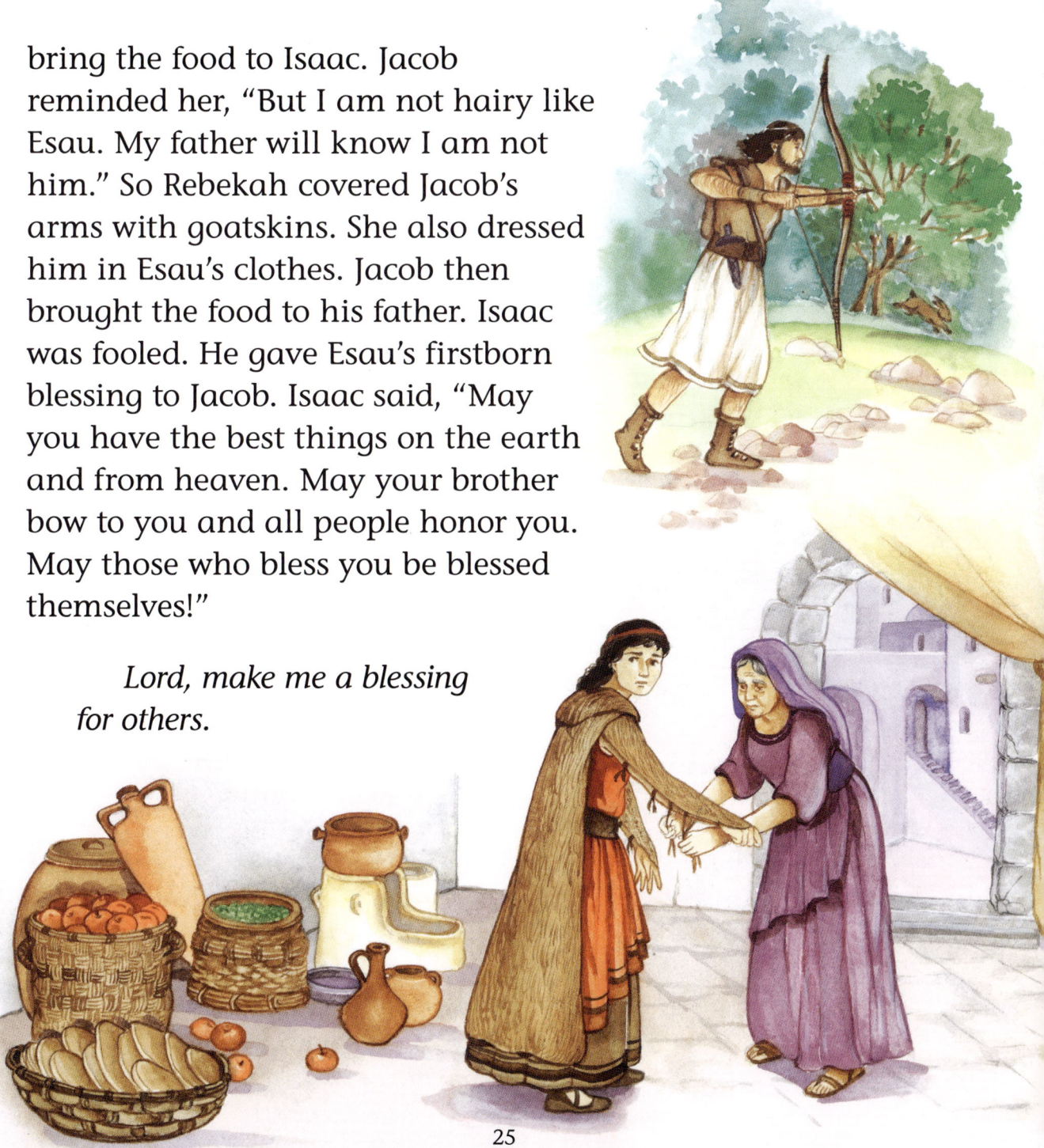

25

# Jacob's Choices

*Genesis 28–29*

When he learned he had been tricked, Esau was angry. He even planned to kill his brother, Jacob. Rebekah told Jacob to run away and live with his uncle Laban. She wanted him to stay there until Esau was no longer angry.

Jacob had to walk alone on his trip. One night when Jacob slept, he

had an amazing dream! A stairway suddenly appeared. Its bottom step rested on the earth, and its top reached all the way to heaven. Angels went up and down on it. Then Jacob heard the Lord say to him, "I am the God of your fathers. I will give you this land. You and your family will be a blessing to everyone." When Jacob woke up he said, "This is an incredible place! It is the gateway to heaven!" And he promised: "If God helps me as I travel, and brings me back home safely, the Lord will be my God."

Jacob finally arrived at his uncle Laban's home. There he met Rachel, Laban's daughter, and fell in love with her. "I want to marry her," Jacob told her father. Laban replied, "After you have worked seven years for me, she will be your wife." So Jacob worked for Laban for seven years.

Finally, the day of the wedding came. The bride wore a special, heavy veil. The morning after the wedding, Jacob found out that his uncle had tricked him. He had not married Rachel but her older sister Leah!

Jacob confronted Laban. "It's not right for the younger to marry first, before her older sister," Laban said. "But in this land one man can have more than one wife. You can marry Rachel if you will work for another seven years."

So Jacob worked another seven years. He loved his new wife, Rachel, very much!

*Lord, help me to be honest in what I say and do.*

# Joseph and the Coat of Many Colors

*Genesis 37*

Jacob had twelve sons, but Joseph was his favorite.

One day Jacob gave Joseph a very special coat. It was made of many colors, not at all like the dull coats his older brothers wore! Joseph's brothers were so jealous they refused to speak to him.

That did not keep Joseph from talking to them. One day, he told them, "Last night I had a strange dream. We were gathering the wheat for the harvest. Suddenly your eleven bundles of wheat bowed down to honor mine!" His brothers were furious. They thought, *Who does Joseph think he is? Is he trying to tell us that he is better than us?*

Things got worse when Joseph told them about his next dream. "I was surrounded by the sun, the moon, and eleven stars," Joseph said, "and they were bowing down to me."

The brothers were fed up with Joseph and his dreams. They began to plot against him. One day when they were herding their flocks away from home, Joseph came out to join them. This was their chance. They ripped off his fancy coat and threw him into a dry, deep well. The brothers were happy about their evil deed. But Reuben, the oldest, secretly planned to rescue Joseph and return him to their father. However, before Reuben could rescue Joseph, traders on their way to Egypt passed by the pit. The other brothers decided to sell Joseph as a slave to these men.

*Lord, give me patience with those who are closest to me, especially my brothers and sisters.*

33

# Joseph in Egypt

*Genesis 39–41*

Joseph became the slave of Potiphar, the captain of Pharaoh's guard. One day Potiphar's wife noticed how handsome Joseph was. She wanted him to sin but he refused. Potiphar's wife then told lies about Joseph, and he was thrown into jail.

Pharaoh's royal baker and butler were also in jail. Each of these men had a strange dream while they were there. When they awoke, they told Joseph about their dreams. Joseph explained to them what each dream meant. The butler would be freed, but the baker would not. Later Joseph's words came true.

One morning two years later, Pharaoh had a scary dream. In it he saw himself by the Nile River. Suddenly seven fat, healthy cows came out of the water. Next came seven sickly cows, which ate the fat cows. Pharaoh then dreamed of seven healthy ears of corn. These were followed by seven ears that were all dried up. Pharaoh wondered what these dreams could mean.

The butler, who had been in jail with Joseph, told Pharaoh, "I know a man who can help you." So the king sent for Joseph. Joseph listened as Pharaoh described his dreams. Then Joseph told him there were going to be seven years of good farming in the land. Those seven good years will be followed by seven years of famine. If Pharaoh prepared for the famine, there would be enough food for all. Pharaoh said, "I can tell that God is with you. You must take care of everything." So Joseph was put in charge of preparing for the famine.

*Lord, help me to always count on you, even in times of trouble.*

# Joseph and His Brothers in Egypt

*Genesis 41–43*

For seven years Joseph set aside food from each harvest. Then came the seven years of famine. "We need food!" the people cried out to Pharaoh.

"Ask Joseph," he told them. "He will help you." Soon, people from all over came to Joseph for food.

In the land of Canaan, Jacob heard that Egypt had extra food. He said to his sons, "Why don't you go to Egypt and buy food for us?" So ten of the brothers went to Egypt. They left the youngest, Benjamin, at home with their father.

When Joseph's brothers arrived, they did not recognize him. He was dressed in the clothes of a powerful Egyptian ruler. Joseph pretended he did not know his brothers. They told him about their youngest brother, Benjamin. They said he was at home. Joseph treated them harshly and called them spies. He gave them food but made them promise to bring Benjamin with them next time, to prove they were telling the truth.

When they returned home, they told Jacob they could only go back again if Benjamin was with them.

Soon they again ran out of food. At first Jacob said, "You cannot take Benjamin to Egypt. I cannot bear to lose him too." But Jacob had no choice. His family needed food. Benjamin would have to go to Egypt with his brothers. They promised to take good care of him and bring back more food for the family.

When they arrived in Egypt, Joseph had his servants bring them to his house to eat lunch. They still did not recognize him. Joseph was very moved to see his youngest brother Benjamin. After a short while, Joseph could no longer control himself. He quickly left the room, so they would not see that he was crying.

Joseph told his servants to fill his brothers' sacks with food. He would not take their payment. He had their money put back into their sacks. Then he told a servant to put his royal cup made of silver into the bag of the youngest brother.

*O Lord, give me the strength to help others in the ways you show me.*

# Hebrews Come to Egypt

*Genesis 44–46*

After their meal, the brothers started home. They were glad they had food to bring back to their father. Suddenly they heard the sound of someone coming after them. They looked at each other in surprise. It was Joseph's servant.

"Why have you done evil?" the servant asked. "Why have you stolen from our master? His silver cup is missing."

The brothers were shocked: "What are you talking about? We would not do such a thing!" One by one, the servant searched each bag. Finally, he reached for the last bag, the one that belonged to Benjamin. To their horror, the cup was found in Benjamin's bag! He would have to be punished!

The brothers returned to Joseph's house and pleaded with him. Joseph announced, "The thief will remain here as my slave. The rest of you may return to your father's house."

Then Judah spoke up, "Please, master, let me speak. If we return without our father's youngest son, it will break his heart. Please keep me as your slave in Benjamin's place."

Joseph could no longer hide his feelings. His brothers had become good men. He ordered his servants to leave. Then he turned and said, "I am Joseph, your brother," and he wept so loudly that the Egyptians heard him.

Joseph's brothers were afraid because they remembered what they had done to him. But Joseph told them, "Do not worry. You sold me into slavery, but God used it to bring about much good. It was God who sent me here to help all these people. Go now and bring my father back. I cannot wait to see him! Bring your families also, for there is enough food for all." Joseph and his brothers embraced and wept for joy.

The brothers returned home with the news, "Joseph is alive!" They loaded up their father, their families, and their livestock to travel to Egypt. There Joseph finally embraced his father, Jacob. Then they settled in the land of Goshen, where their families grew.

*Lord, help me to trust your plan for me, even when things are not clear or easy.*

# Moses Is Born

### Exodus 1–2

In Egypt, Jacob's family members were known as Hebrews or Israelites. They prospered in Egypt.

Many years after Joseph died, there was a new Pharaoh. He knew nothing about Joseph and how God had used him to provide food for the people during the famine. Pharaoh only saw how strong and numerous the Hebrews were. He was afraid that they might try to take over Egypt. So Pharaoh forced the Hebrews to become slaves.

The number of Hebrews continued to grow and Pharaoh become more and more worried. He gave an evil order to his soldiers: "When a baby boy is born to the Israelites, throw him into the river. Let the girls live."

One Hebrew family had a baby boy. They did not want him to be killed. They hid him in a basket on the bank of the river. His sister watched from the tall grass to see what would happen

46

to him. Pharaoh's daughter came to the river to swim. She heard the baby's cries and sent one of her servants to get him. "He must be a Hebrew baby," she said. "Look, he's crying. He must be hungry."

The baby's sister stepped forward. "I could get one of the Hebrew women to nurse him for you," she said. Pharaoh's daughter agreed to this, so the girl ran home and got her mother. "Take care of him for me," Pharaoh's daughter told her. "When he is a little older, I will adopt him." Pharaoh's daughter named the boy Moses, which means "I drew him out of the water."

*Lord, help me protect the life of every person, no matter how old or how young.*

47

# The Burning Bush

*Exodus 3–4*

As the adopted son of Pharaoh's daughter, Moses was a prince in Egypt. Even so, he was troubled by the suffering the Hebrews experienced as slaves. One day he saw an Egyptian beating a Hebrew. Moses became so angry that he killed the Egyptian and hid his body in the sand. Word got out that Moses had killed the Egyptian. Pharaoh would have to punish him with death. So Moses fled Egypt and went to a land called Midian.

Moses began a new life in Midian. He married, had a son, and became a shepherd, watching over his family's flocks. One day, he took the sheep to the mountain of Horeb. There, Moses saw something very strange. A bush was on fire, but the fire was not consuming the bush. When Moses drew closer, he heard a voice call out to him, "Moses! Moses!"

He answered, "Here I am."

The voice from the fiery bush said, "Take off your shoes. You are on ground that is holy." Moses knelt and removed his shoes. Then the voice continued: "I am the God of your fathers, of Abraham, Isaac, and Jacob." Moses was afraid to look at God, so he hid his face. God said, "I have seen the misery of my people. I will rescue them and bring them to a place flowing with milk and honey. You will lead the Israelites out of Egypt."

Moses was shocked. He knew that the Israelites were slaves. But he wondered how he

could possibly lead them out of Egypt. He asked, "How will I be able to do this?"

"I will be with you," God promised.

Then Moses realized the Hebrews would have questions too. He asked God, "What will I say to the Israelites when they ask who sent me?"

God answered, "I AM WHO AM. You will tell them that 'I AM' has sent you to lead them to freedom."

Moses was still afraid. "You should get someone else," he said. "I cannot speak well. Nobody will listen to me."

God was angry that Moses did not trust him. But God told Moses, "Aaron, your brother, will go with you and do some of the speaking. But you will lead the people, and I will be with you."

Moses obeyed God and returned to Egypt.

*O God, give me courage to do whatever you ask of me. I know that you will be with me to help me.*

# The First Nine Plagues

*Exodus 5–11*

Moses told Aaron everything God had said to him from the burning bush. God heard their prayers and was going to save Israel! The brothers took the news to the people, and everyone gave thanks to God. Then Moses and Aaron went to Pharaoh.

"The God of Israel wants you to let his people go," said the brothers.

"Who is this god that I should obey him?" asked Pharaoh. He sent them away and punished the Israelites by giving them more work. So the Israelites blamed Moses and Aaron for making things worse!

God told Moses not to worry. "I will make Pharaoh set my people free," God said. "Go back to Pharaoh. When he asks for proof that I sent you, tell Aaron to throw his staff to the ground. I will turn the staff into a snake."

Moses and Aaron returned to Pharaoh. When Pharaoh asked for a sign, Moses told Aaron to throw down his staff. It became a giant snake! Still, Pharaoh was not impressed. He called his magicians, and they also made their staffs turn into snakes. Aaron's snake quickly swallowed the magicians' snakes, but Pharaoh still refused to listen. So the brothers left Pharaoh's court.

The next morning, God told Moses, "Go to the bank of the Nile River. You will find Pharaoh there. Say to him, 'The Lord told you to let his people go, but you did not listen. I have come with a sign from the Lord to show that God is with Israel.' Then tell Aaron to strike the river with his staff. I will turn it

into blood." Moses and Aaron did as God commanded. The river turned red with blood, but Pharaoh still would not listen.

God sent more terrible plagues upon Egypt. The next time Moses told Aaron to raise his staff, a horde of frogs invaded the land. Then gnats and flies swarmed over Egypt, and a terrible disease broke out that killed many animals. Next, a

fine dust settled on the people and left awful blisters on their skin. Hail fell from the sky and ruined the crops. A thick cloud of locusts ate every plant in sight. Finally, God sent three days of darkness. No one could

see or move around. The Egyptians suffered greatly, but God kept Israel safe from every plague. Still, Pharaoh refused to listen to God.

*Lord, thank you for listening to my prayers. Help me to listen to you, too, when you want to show me what is right and good.*

# The First Passover

*Exodus 12*

Pharaoh refused to listen to God. So God told Moses, "I am sending a tenth plague. This one will make Pharaoh set my people free.

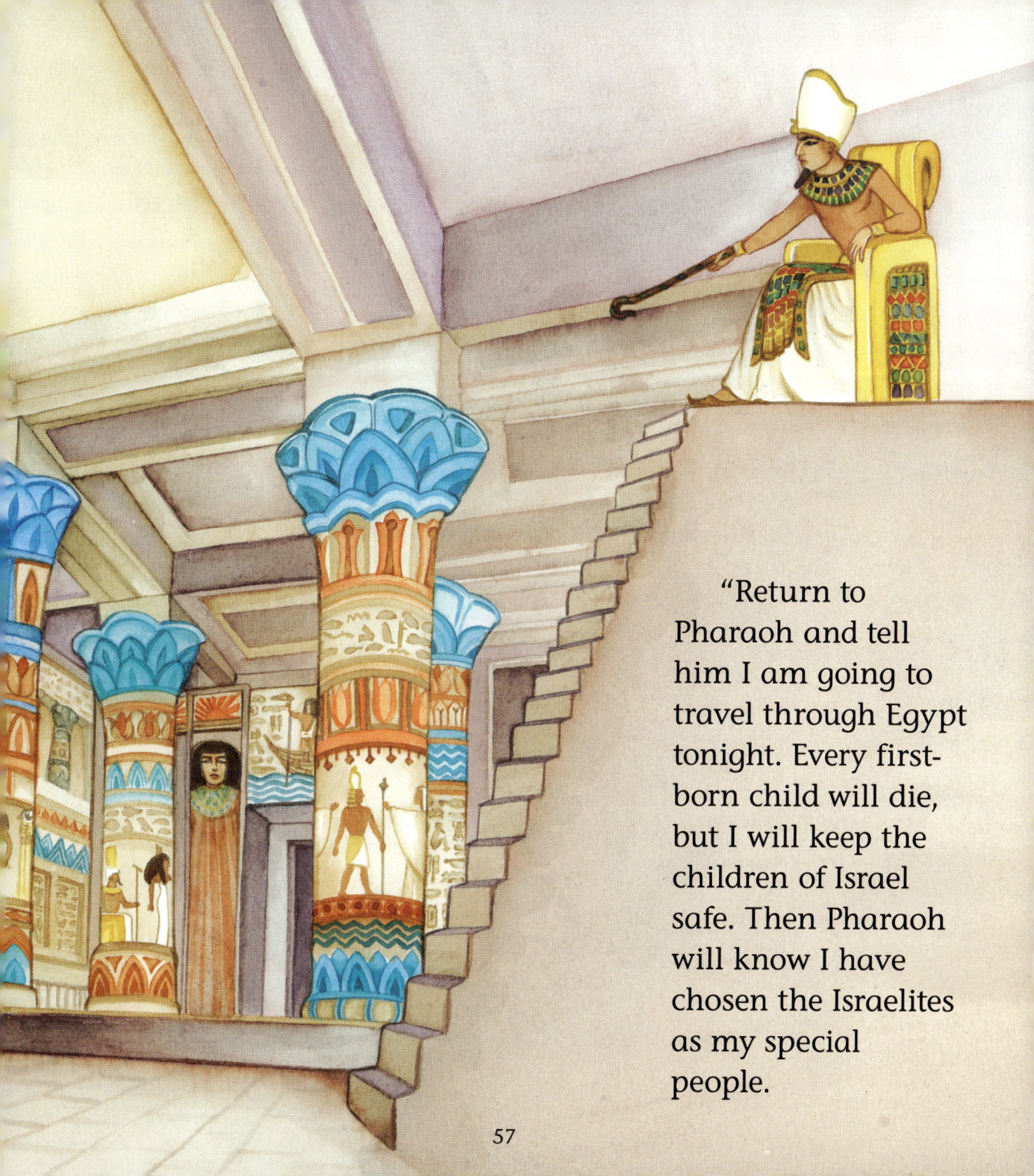

"Return to Pharaoh and tell him I am going to travel through Egypt tonight. Every first-born child will die, but I will keep the children of Israel safe. Then Pharaoh will know I have chosen the Israelites as my special people.

"Tell every family in Israel to get a lamb for supper, roast it, and eat it quickly. You must also tell each household to paint the doorposts of their homes with blood from the lamb.

"At midnight, I will visit every home in Egypt. All the first-born children of the Egyptians will die.

But when I see lamb's blood on the door of a house, I will pass over it. Everyone inside that house will be safe.

"You will always remember this night as the 'Passover' of the Lord. Celebrate this Passover every year to remember how I freed you from slavery in Egypt."

*Lord, I bless your name.*
*You always answer me when*
*I ask for help.*

# The Red Sea

## *Exodus 14*

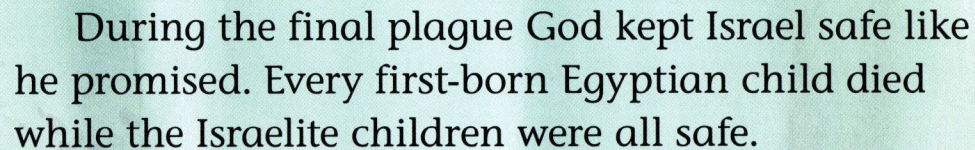

During the final plague God kept Israel safe like he promised. Every first-born Egyptian child died while the Israelite children were all safe.

When Pharaoh saw this, he immediately called Moses and Aaron. "Take your people and go!" he cried. The Israelites fled at once. God led them along the safest paths. He went before them as a cloud by day. At night, he was a tower of fire.

The moment Pharaoh heard Israel was gone, he regretted sending them away. "Who will work if I have no slaves?" he asked. He called his army and ordered them to stop the Israelites.

Moses and the people were by the Red Sea when they heard Pharaoh and his army approaching. The people panicked. "Moses, what have you done?" they asked. "You brought us here to die!"

Moses answered, "Do not fear. God will protect us." Then he prayed to God for help.

God said to Moses, "Raise your staff over the sea. I will divide the waters so you can cross the sea on dry land." Moses obeyed. Then God parted the waters and led Israel across the sea. Pharaoh tried to follow them, but God told Moses, "Raise your staff again." Moses did, and the sea flowed back over the Egyptians. Israel was free! The people blessed God for saving them.

*Lord, thank you for the*
*wonderful things you have done.*

# Manna from Heaven

*Exodus 16–17*

When Israel left Egypt, they traveled through the wilderness for many weeks. Soon they were very hungry. "We should have stayed in Egypt!" they complained to Moses and Aaron. "We are dying of hunger!"

God heard their cries and spoke to Moses. "I will give you bread from heaven every morning," he promised. "At night, I will provide meat. Then you will know that I am your God."

That evening, God sent quail into Israel's camp. At dawn, he covered the ground with soft white bread. It was

wafer-thin and sweet as honey.
"What is this?" the Israelites asked
Moses.

"This is the bread God is giving
you," Moses answered. "Every
generation of Israel must remember
how God fed us in the wilderness."
The Israelites called the bread "manna."

Later, the people grew very thirsty. God spoke to Moses
again, saying, "Take your staff and strike the rock before you."
Moses obeyed, and fresh water poured out for everyone to drink.
God cared for his people in this way until they reached the land
he had promised them.

*God, you know what I need, even before I ask you for something.*
*I want to share all my needs with you!*

# The Ten Commandments

*Exodus 19–20*

The Israelites traveled for months after leaving Egypt. When they reached the desert of Sinai, they set up camp. There God spoke to Moses on the mountain.

"You have seen me rescue you from Pharaoh. If you obey me and keep my commandments, I will make you my holy and special people.

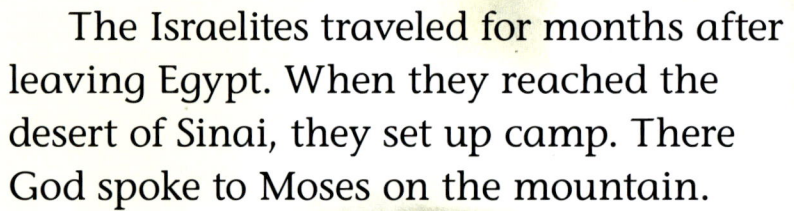

"I am God, who saved you. Do not have any god but me.

"My name is holy. Do not use it carelessly.

"Keep the Sabbath as my holy day.

"Honor your father and mother.

"Do not kill.

"Do not have impure relationships.

"Do not steal.

"Do not lie or gossip.

"Do not desire your neighbor's wife.

"Do not envy the good things your neighbor has."

*God, thank you for making me a member of your Church. I am one of your special people! Help me to live as your child by following the law you gave us.*

# Ruth

*Ruth 1–4*

Israel settled in Canaan, the land God promised to give them. But the Israelites quickly forgot their covenant with God.

Centuries later, Canaan was hit by famine, and many Israelites left. One man, Elimelech, took his family to Moab to look for food. But tragedy followed them. Elimelech and his sons died there, leaving his widow, Naomi, and her Moabite daughters-in-law Orpah and Ruth all alone.

Naomi told her daughters-in-law, "I will return to Canaan. But you must stay in Moab with your own people."

Ruth refused to leave Naomi's side. "I will stay with you," she told Naomi. "Your people and your God will be my own."

Ruth went to Canaan with Naomi. There, she married Boaz and gave birth to a son, Obed. Obed would be the grandfather of David, the future king of Israel.

*God, bless all who need your help today.*

# Samuel

*1 Samuel 1–3*

In the days of Ruth and Boaz, there was a woman named Hannah living in the nearby region of Ephraim. Hannah and her husband, Elkanah, traveled to the Lord's temple at Shiloh every year to pray.

One year, Hannah entered the temple crying. "Lord, see how miserable I am," she prayed. "I have no children, but I want a child so badly. If you give me a son, I promise to dedicate him to you."

Eli the priest watched Hannah pray. He approached her and gave her a blessing, saying, "Go in peace! May God answer your prayer." Hannah left and returned home.

Soon, God blessed Hannah with a
baby boy! She named him Samuel.
When Samuel was old enough, Hannah
brought him to the temple and left him
in the care of Eli. Samuel would belong
to God, just as Hannah had promised.

Years later, when Samuel was a young boy, a voice called to him while he was sleeping in the temple. "Samuel! Samuel!" said the voice. Samuel ran to Eli and said, "Here I am! You called me."

But Eli had not called Samuel. "Go back to sleep," he told the boy.

Samuel obeyed, but the voice returned. He ran to Eli two more times. Then Eli realized the Lord was calling Samuel.

"Go back to sleep," Eli said. "If God calls you again, say, 'Speak, Lord. Your servant is listening.'"

Samuel returned to bed. When the Lord called him, Samuel answered: "Speak, Lord. I am listening!"

*God, you hear every prayer I say. Help me hear you, too, especially when I read your word.*

71

# Saul

*1 Samuel 8–13*

Samuel grew up, and God was with him. Samuel listened to the Lord and spoke his words to the people of Israel. Everyone loved Samuel and trusted him as their leader.

When Samuel grew old, he named his two sons leaders of Israel. But his sons were selfish and did not love the Lord. When

the Israelites saw this, they approached Samuel and begged, "Give us a king so we can be like other nations!"

Samuel was worried. Was not God himself the king of Israel? But the Lord said to Samuel, "The people have rejected me. Give them the king they ask for."

Then the Lord chose Saul to be Israel's king.

*God, when I ask you for help, you will show me what is right.*

# David and Goliath

*1 Samuel 16–17*

King Saul won many battles for Israel, but he did not follow the Lord. Samuel saw this and regretted making Saul king. Then God said to Samuel, "I have chosen a new leader for my people. Go to Bethlehem and find Jesse, son of Obed. You will anoint one of his sons king."

Samuel found Jesse and met his oldest son, Eliab. "This must be our future king," Samuel thought.

"No," the Lord said, "not him. You judge by his looks, but I see the heart."

Then Samuel met six more of Jesse's sons, but God chose none of them. "Do you have any more sons?" Samuel asked Jesse.

Jesse answered, "There is one more. David, my youngest, is watching the sheep."

"Call him," said Samuel.

When David arrived, God told Samuel, "Here he is! Anoint him." From that day, the Lord was with David in a special way.

A short time later, the Philistine army marched against Israel. King Saul gathered his soldiers, including three of David's brothers, and went to meet the Philistines. When they arrived, Goliath, the champion of the Philistine army, stepped forward. "Choose someone to fight me!" he cried. He continued, "If he wins, we will be your slaves. If I win, you will be our slaves." But Israel trembled. No one was brave enough to fight.

Forty days passed. Jesse sent David to see how the battle was going. When David heard Goliath's challenge, he approached Saul. "Let me fight," David said. "God saved me from bears and lions when I watched my father's sheep. He will protect me here, too!" Saul agreed to let the young man fight.

David took a staff, sling, and five smooth stones, and walked toward Goliath. "I fight in the name of the God of Israel!" he cried. He drew back his sling and killed Goliath with a single shot.

David became a hero in Israel that day. All the people sang of his courage.

*God, you have chosen me for a special mission, just like you chose David. Help me discover and live your great plans for me!*

# David the King

*1 Samuel 18–31; 2 Samuel*

Israel praised David for killing Goliath and winning many battles. Because of this, King Saul became jealous. "Soon they will make David king instead of me!" he said. So he wanted to have David killed.

When David found out his life was in danger, he went into hiding. His friends told him to fight back, but David still respected King Saul. "I have no right to hurt him," David said. "God chose him to be king. He is God's anointed one."

Years later, war broke out between the Philistines and Israel. The Philistines attacked and killed Saul, and drove Israel from their land. David and his men wept for Saul and for their people.

The surviving Israelites made David king. David worked hard to serve God and his people.

*God, you are my king. Help me serve you with love.*

# Elijah

*1 Kings 16–17*

David ruled Israel for forty years. After his death, one king after another rose to lead God's people, but they did not love the Lord as David had. They broke God's commandments and worshiped false gods.

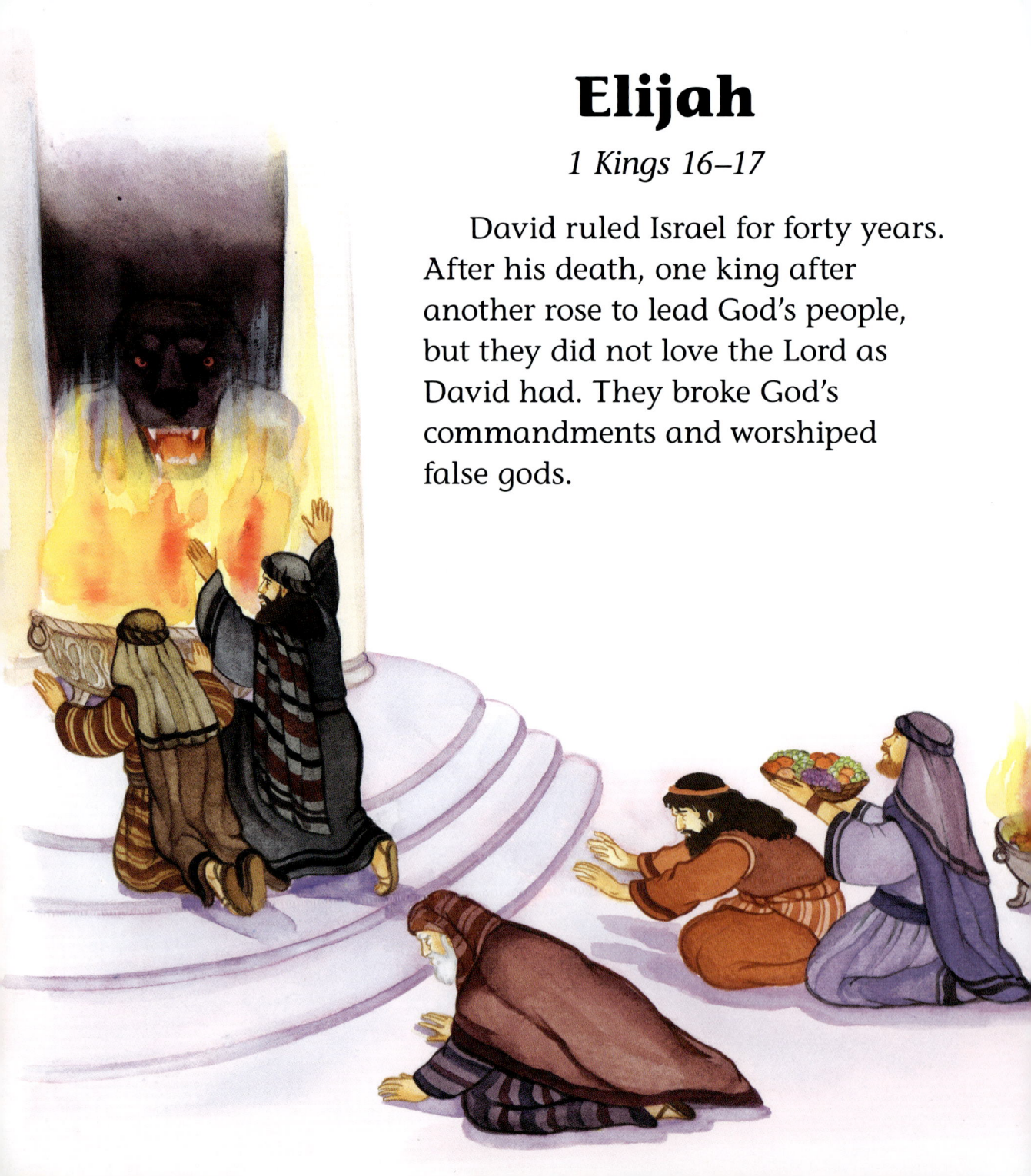

King Ahab was the worst. Ahab built an altar to a false god named Baal and encouraged Israel to pray there. Soon, the Israelites forgot the Lord who had rescued them from Egypt.

When God saw this, he sent Elijah, his prophet, to speak to Ahab. "The Lord says there will be no rain in the coming years," Elijah told the king. For the next three years, the rains stopped. The riverbed dried up and the crops and animals died. Israel began to starve.

But God took care of Elijah. "Go to Zarephath," God told his prophet. "I have asked a widow to feed you there."

When Elijah reached Zarephath, he saw a woman collecting sticks by the town gate. "Please give me a drink of water and some bread," he asked her.

"God knows I have no bread to give you," she answered. "I only have a little flour and oil. I am about to bake a small loaf of bread with them. After my son and I eat it, we will die, for this is all the food we have left."

"Do not be afraid," Elijah said. "Bring me something to eat first. The Lord says you will not run out of flour and oil until he sends rain upon Israel again."

The widow did as Elijah said. Her flour and oil did not run out, and she and her son ate for many days.

*Lord, you are always taking care of me. May I always trust in you!*

# Elijah and the Prophets of Baal

*1 Kings 18*

After Elijah spoke God's word to King Ahab, Israel suffered three years without rain. Then Elijah returned to the king. "Is that you, Elijah?" Ahab shouted. "The troublemaker of Israel?"

"I did not cause this drought," Elijah answered. "You are suffering because you left the Lord to worship false gods. Now, I want you to gather the Israelites and the prophets of Baal and meet me at Mount Carmel."

When Ahab had done so, Elijah spoke to them. "How long will you worship multiple gods? Make up your mind and choose one! If the Lord is God, then follow him. If Baal is God, follow him." The people stayed silent.

Elijah continued. "I am the only prophet of the Lord. There are 450 prophets of Baal here. Let each of us prepare one bull for sacrifice. You will pray to your gods, and I will pray to the Lord. The god who starts the fire for our sacrifice is the true god."

Baal's prophets prepared their sacrifice first. They cried to Baal all morning and into the afternoon, but nothing happened. Then Elijah stepped forward. "Come closer," he told the people, "and pour water on the sacrifice I have prepared here." When everything was

dripping wet, Elijah prayed, "Lord, show your people that you are their God. Turn their hearts back to you." The Lord sent fire down at once. It consumed everything, even the water on the ground!

"The Lord is God! The Lord is God!" the people cried, and they worshiped him.

*God, I love you and believe in you. Help me follow you always!*

# Isaiah

*Isaiah 6–7*

God loved Israel as a father loves his child. But Israel still wandered from the Lord and disobeyed him. So God chose Isaiah, son of Amoz, to be the next prophet to his people.

God appeared to Isaiah as a great king seated on a throne and surrounded by angels. Isaiah was frightened by this vision.

"How can I look at you?" Isaiah asked God. "I am not worthy. I am a sinner, just like everyone else in Israel."

At that, an angel approached Isaiah and touched his lips with a burning coal. "With this, your sins are gone," the angel said.

Then Isaiah heard the voice of God. "Who will I send to speak to Israel?"

"Here I am," Isaiah answered. "Send me." So God sent Isaiah to Ahaz, King of Judah.

At that
time, Ahaz was
preparing to defend
Israel from Syrian
invaders. He was terribly afraid.

Isaiah said to him, "The Lord says, 'Do not
fear. Have faith, and I will deliver you. This is
how you will know that I am about to save
you: a young woman will have a baby boy
and name him Emmanuel.'"

Isaiah also spoke about a future king. This
king would descend from David and bring
peace and justice to Israel forever.

*God, please forgive me when I sin. Then fill me
with your life so I can share your love with others.*

# Jonah

*Jonah 1–4*

In the days of Jeroboam II, King of Israel, the Lord spoke to his prophet Jonah. "Go to the big city of Nineveh and tell the people there to stop doing evil," he said.

Jonah did not want to go to Nineveh. Instead, he tried to run from the presence of the Lord. He found a boat headed for Tarshish and got on board.

Then God sent a great storm upon the sea. The mighty winds tossed the boat back and forth, until the sailors feared it would break into pieces. The captain found Jonah fast asleep below deck. "Why are you sleeping?" he shouted. "Get up and pray to your God! Maybe he will save us!"

As Jonah rose, the rest of the crew began to question him. "Why has this storm come upon us?" they asked. "Who are you, and where are you from?"

"I am a Hebrew," Jonah answered. "My God is the one who made the land and the sea. I am running away from his presence."

The sailors trembled in fear. "How could you do this?" they cried. They could hear the storm growing louder and more violent. "What can we do to quiet down the storm?"

"Throw me overboard," Jonah replied. "This storm is my fault." The sailors hesitated. They tried to row harder, but the winds only grew worse. Finally, they grabbed Jonah and prepared to throw him into the sea. "Lord, please do not punish us for this!" they cried, and they threw Jonah overboard. The storm stopped at once. From that moment on, the sailors worshiped the God of Israel.

—◦—◦—◦—

Meanwhile, God sent a giant fish to swallow Jonah. He spent three days and three nights in the fish's belly. Jonah thanked God for saving him, saying, "I sank into the waters, but you heard my prayer and rescued me. I thank you, my God. You are the one who saves!" After three days, God told the fish to spit Jonah out onto dry land.

Again the Lord spoke to Jonah. "Go to the big city of Nineveh. Give them my message." This time, Jonah obeyed. He began the long walk through Nineveh, shouting the message God had given him: "In forty days, Nineveh will be destroyed!" When the people heard these words, they began to fast and pray. Even the king of Nineveh refused to eat or drink anything, but prayed wholeheartedly to God for forgiveness. God saw their change of heart. He had mercy and did not punish them.

This made Jonah very angry. "Lord, I knew you would do this!" he said. "This is exactly why I tried to run from you! I knew you were kind and merciful, ready to forgive even the people of Nineveh. But these people are our enemies! They have fought against your people, Israel. They do not worship you as God!"

"Is it right for you to be angry?" God asked.

Jonah said nothing, but went and sat on a hill looking over the city to see what would happen next. The sun grew hot overhead, so the Lord sent a shady plant to protect and comfort Jonah. The next day, the plant died. Jonah grew hot and dizzy from the blazing sun and was angry that his shade had been taken from him.

"Is it right for you to be angry about losing your shade plant?" God asked again.

"Yes!" Jonah replied.

God answered, "You are concerned about a plant, which you neither created nor worked to take care of. Should I not be concerned about this great city and its people, over one hundred and twenty thousand of them?"

*God, help me treat everyone with respect and patience.*

# Judas Maccabeus

*1 Maccabees*

Three hundred years before Christ was born, Alexander the Great rose to power. He built an army and conquered many nations. Then he got very sick. Before Alexander died, he divided his empire among his best military officers.

The officers crowned themselves kings and used their power for evil. One of them, King Antiochus, invaded Jerusalem.

He entered the Temple of the Jews and stole the golden lampstand, the altars, and everything the Israelites used to worship God. Two years later, Antiochus made a terrible law. "From now on, everyone must worship the gods I give you," he wrote. "If you disobey, you will die."

Mattathias, a priest of Israel, was troubled. "I will not obey this law," he declared. "Even if every nation follows Antiochus, my family and I will serve the Lord!" He urged others to join him. "If you

95

love God's law, follow me!" he said. Then Mattathias and his family left the city. Many Israelites followed them. They settled in the desert where they could freely worship God. Mattathias spent the rest of his years in the desert. Before he died, he told Israel to keep fighting for their right to worship God. "If you trust in the Lord, he will give you strength to follow his law!" he said. Then Mattathias appointed his son Judas Maccabeus to lead the people after his death.

After many more years in the desert, Israel finally got a chance to take back the Temple from their enemies. Judas and the people prepared for battle by praying and fasting. They prayed, "Lord God, how can we win this fight if you do not help us? Remember the covenant you made with our fathers. Protect us!"

God heard his people. The Israelites won a great victory. They took back the Temple, cleaned and purified it, and built a new altar. Then they offered everything to God.

For eight days, the people sang, danced, and blessed God for his goodness. Their joy was so great, they decided to hold this eight-day celebration every year to thank God for all he had done for them.

*God, thank you for giving us a special place, your Church, where we can worship you in freedom.*

# New Testament

# An Angel Visits Mary

*Luke 1*

God sent his angel Gabriel to the town of Nazareth with a special message for a young girl who lived there. Her name was Mary.

Gabriel greeted Mary with joy. "Hail, full of grace!" he said. "The Lord is with you."

Mary did not understand the angel's words. "Do not be afraid, Mary," Gabriel continued. "God has chosen you. You will

have a son and name him Jesus. He will rule over the people of Israel forever."

"How can this happen?" Mary asked. "I am not married yet."

"The Holy Spirit will come upon you, and the power of God will cover you with his shadow," Gabriel told her. "Your child will be the Son of God. Your cousin Elizabeth is also going to have a son, even though she and her husband Zechariah thought this was impossible. Truly, nothing is impossible for God."

Mary answered, "Let this happen to me, just as you have said." Then Gabriel left her.

*God, help me say "yes" to your plans for me, like Mary did.*

# Mary Visits Elizabeth

*Luke 1*

When Mary heard that her cousin Elizabeth was going to have a son, she left Nazareth at once to visit her.

The moment Elizabeth heard Mary's voice, she was filled with the Holy Spirit and felt her baby jump for joy inside of her. "Blessed are you among women!" Elizabeth exclaimed. "And how blessed is the child growing inside of you! Who am I, that the mother of my Lord should visit me? You are truly blessed for believing God's words!"

Mary answered with a song of praise. "My soul sings of God's greatness. I rejoice in God, my savior! God does great things for me, and his name is holy. He has remembered the promise he made to his people Israel." Mary stayed with Elizabeth for three months. Then she went home to Nazareth.

*God, thank you for the great things you have done for me!*

# Jesus Is Born

*Luke 2; Matthew 2*

In the days before Jesus was born, the Roman emperor ordered everyone to return to their native city. They were to be counted and registered. Mary's husband, Joseph, was a descendant of David. So he and Mary made the long journey from Nazareth to the city of David, called Bethlehem.

While they were there, Mary and Joseph looked for a place to stay, but the inn was full. The only shelter was a stable for animals. Mary and Joseph decided to settle there. Then the time came for Mary to have her baby boy. She gave birth to Jesus, wrapped him in swaddling clothes, and laid him in a manger.

Meanwhile, several shepherds were watching their sheep in a nearby field. Suddenly an angel appeared to them. "I bring great and joyful news, for you and for all people!" the angel said.

"Today a savior has been born for you in Bethlehem. You will find him lying in a manger." When the angel finished speaking, an entire host of angels appeared and blessed God, saying, "Glory to God in heaven, and peace to people on earth!"

When the angels had left them, the shepherds said to one another, "Let's go see this for ourselves!" They immediately set out for Bethlehem. They found the stable with Mary, Joseph, and baby Jesus. Jesus was lying in a manger, just as the angel had said.

Three wise men from the East also heard about Jesus' birth. They saw a star that was much brighter than usual and knew this was a sign that the king had been born. The wise men packed gifts of gold, frankincense, and myrrh for the baby king. They followed the star to the stable in Bethlehem. When the wise men saw Jesus, they knelt, worshiped, and gave him their precious gifts. Then they went back to their own countries.

I praise you,
O Lord, together
with all your
angels!

# The Presentation of Jesus

*Luke 2*

Forty days after Jesus' birth, Mary and Joseph brought him to the Temple to present him to the Lord. While they were there, the Holy Spirit inspired a man named Simeon to approach them.

Simeon was a holy man who trusted God deeply. Because of this, God promised Simeon that he would not die before seeing the Messiah, the savior of Israel. When Simeon saw Mary, Joseph, and baby Jesus, he knew Jesus was the promised Messiah. "Lord, you have kept your word!" Simeon exclaimed.

He took Jesus into his arms and held him. "Now, I can die in peace. I have seen salvation and light for the whole world."

Then Simeon looked at Mary. "Many people will reject this child," he told her.

Simeon's words amazed Mary and Joseph. Mary kept them in her heart.

*God, teach me to trust in your word. You have power to save us!*

# Jesus Found in the Temple

*Luke 2*

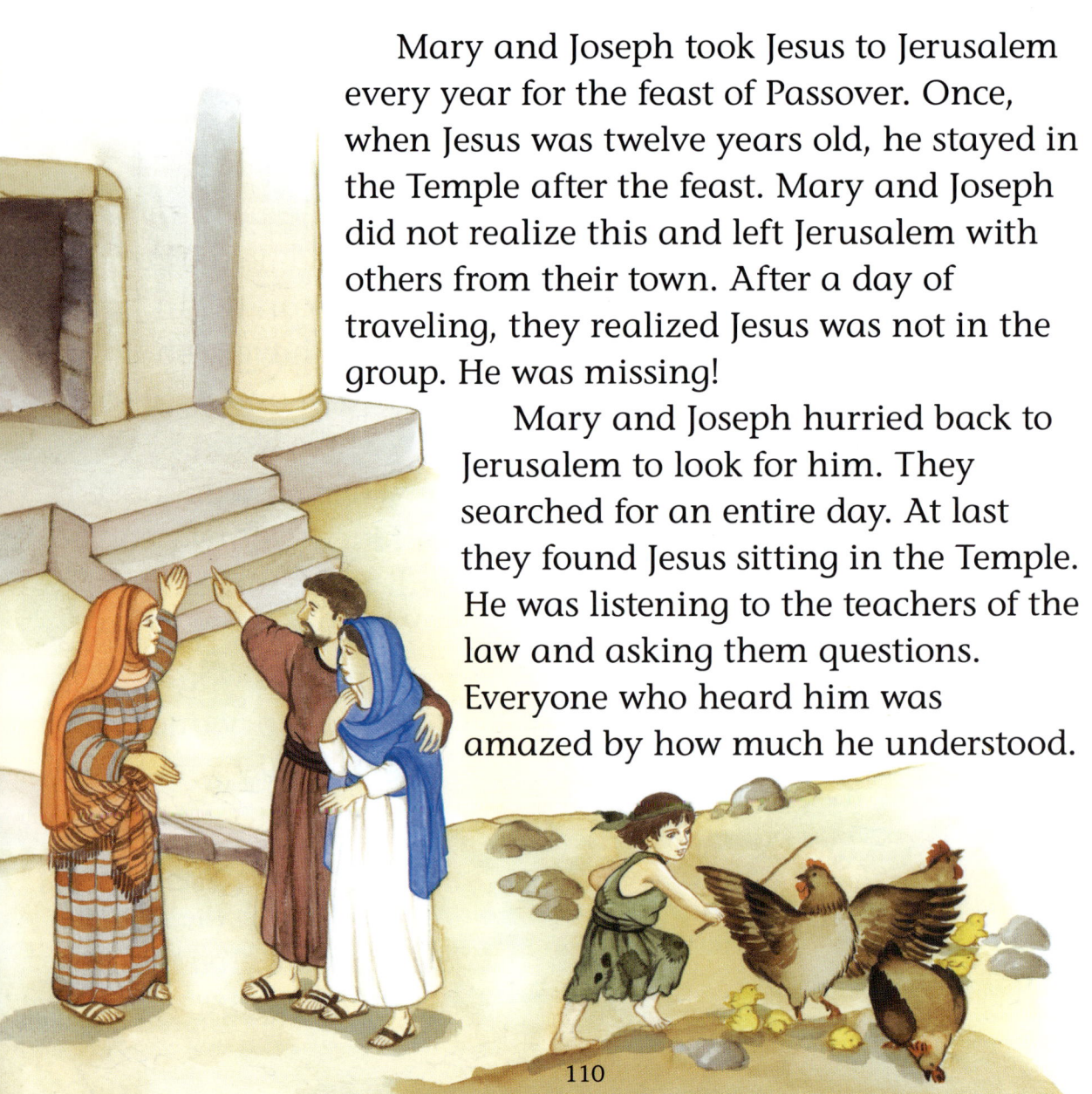

Mary and Joseph took Jesus to Jerusalem every year for the feast of Passover. Once, when Jesus was twelve years old, he stayed in the Temple after the feast. Mary and Joseph did not realize this and left Jerusalem with others from their town. After a day of traveling, they realized Jesus was not in the group. He was missing!

Mary and Joseph hurried back to Jerusalem to look for him. They searched for an entire day. At last they found Jesus sitting in the Temple. He was listening to the teachers of the law and asking them questions. Everyone who heard him was amazed by how much he understood.

Mary and Joseph were also amazed. Mary said to Jesus, "Why have you done this to us? Your father and I were so worried. We looked everywhere for you!"

Jesus replied, "Why were you looking for me? Didn't you know I would be in my Father's house?" Mary and Joseph did not understand his words.

Jesus left the Temple with his parents and returned home to Nazareth. He grew up listening to Mary and Joseph and obeying them. Mary also listened to Jesus. She reflected on all his words and kept them in her heart.

*God, please guide my parents in all they do, and help me to obey them.*

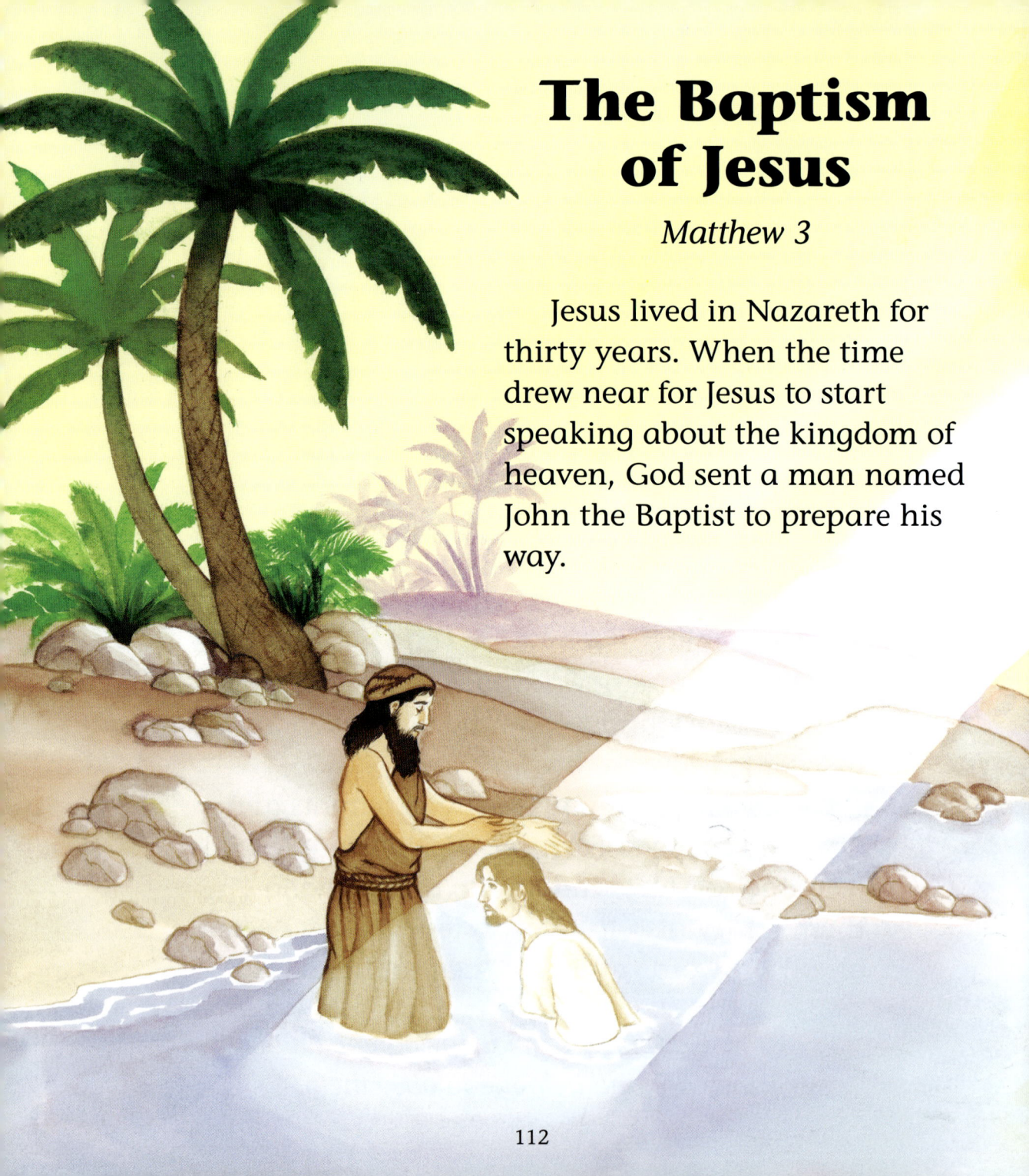

# The Baptism of Jesus

*Matthew 3*

Jesus lived in Nazareth for thirty years. When the time drew near for Jesus to start speaking about the kingdom of heaven, God sent a man named John the Baptist to prepare his way.

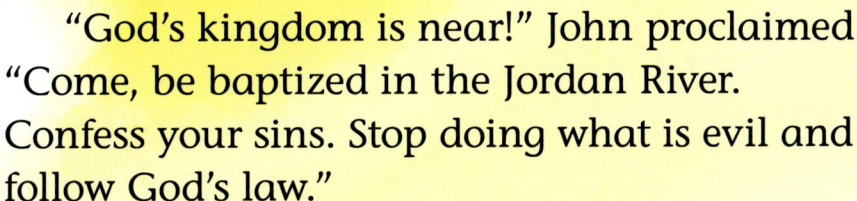

"God's kingdom is near!" John proclaimed.
"Come, be baptized in the Jordan River.
Confess your sins. Stop doing what is evil and
follow God's law."

One day, while John was preaching, Jesus
came to him for baptism. John was amazed
and tried to prevent him. "I need to be
baptized by you!" John exclaimed. "Why come
to me?"

Jesus answered, "Let it happen this way. We
must follow God's plan."

John baptized Jesus. When he finished,
Jesus stood and saw the heavens open. The
Holy Spirit came upon him like a dove, and a
voice from heaven said, "This is my Son. I love
him and am pleased with him."

*Lord, I believe that you love me. Teach me how
I can show my love for you every day.*

# The Temptation of Jesus

### *Matthew 4*

After his baptism, Jesus went to the desert
for forty days of prayer and fasting. Afterward,
he was very hungry.

The devil saw this and said, "If you are
God's Son, tell these rocks to turn into bread."

"We do not live by only eating bread. We live by following God's Word," Jesus replied.

Then the devil took Jesus to the Temple in Jerusalem. "If you are God's Son, throw yourself off the Temple roof," he said. "Scripture says God will send angels to catch you."

Jesus answered, "Scripture also says, 'Do not test God!'"

Finally, the devil showed Jesus the great kingdoms of the world. "Worship me, and I will give these to you," he said.

"Go away, Satan!" Jesus said. "We must worship God alone!" Then the devil left, and angels appeared to care for Jesus.

*Lord, help me remember your words when I am tempted to do something wrong.*

# The Call of the Disciples

*Luke 4–6*

Huge crowds came to hear Jesus speak. One day, Jesus borrowed a boat from a fisherman named Simon and rowed a short distance offshore. He taught from the water while the people stood on land, so the people could see and hear him better.

When Jesus finished teaching, he turned to Simon, who was sitting in the boat with him. "Go into deep water and catch some fish," he said.

"Teacher, I worked all night and caught nothing!" Simon answered. "But if you say so, I will try again."

Simon found James and John, his fishing partners, and returned to sea. This time they caught so many fish, their boat began to sink!

The three fishermen finally got the fish and their boat safely to shore. Immediately, Simon went to Jesus and fell at his feet. "Lord, go away from me. I am a sinful man," he said.

Jesus said to Simon, "Do not be afraid. From now on, you will catch people, not fish."

That day, Simon, James, and John left everything and followed Jesus.

Jesus continued calling disciples. Then, on a night when all were fast asleep, he went up a mountain to pray. He spent the whole night in prayer with his Father. At dawn, he came down from the mountain and chose twelve men to follow him more closely. He named them Apostles. Their names were: Simon Peter, Andrew, James, John, Philip, Bartholomew, Matthew, Thomas, James the son of Alpheus, Simon the Zealot, Judas the son of James, and Judas Iscariot.

*Jesus, I will listen to your words and learn from you.*

# The Wedding at Cana

*John 2*

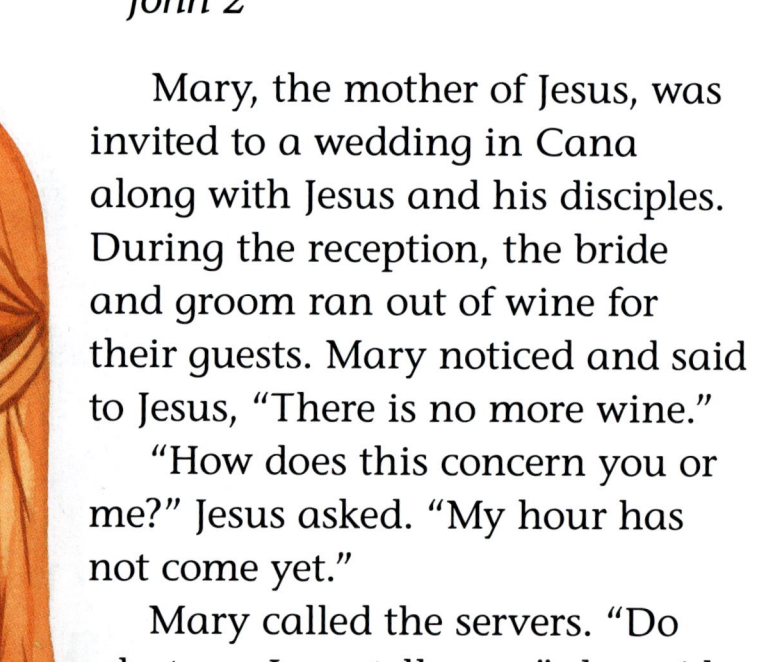

Mary, the mother of Jesus, was invited to a wedding in Cana along with Jesus and his disciples. During the reception, the bride and groom ran out of wine for their guests. Mary noticed and said to Jesus, "There is no more wine."

"How does this concern you or me?" Jesus asked. "My hour has not come yet."

Mary called the servers. "Do whatever Jesus tells you," she said to them.

Now there were six stone jars nearby. Jesus told the servers, "Fill those jars with water and take them to the head waiter." The servers obeyed. When the head waiter drank from one of the jars, he tasted wine!

The waiter called the bride and groom at once. "Most people serve the best wine first at their wedding," he told them. "But you have saved the best wine for last!"

This was Jesus' first miracle. When his disciples saw this, they believed in him.

*Jesus, I believe you always want the best for me. Thank you for giving me all I have!*

# The Woman at the Well

*John 4*

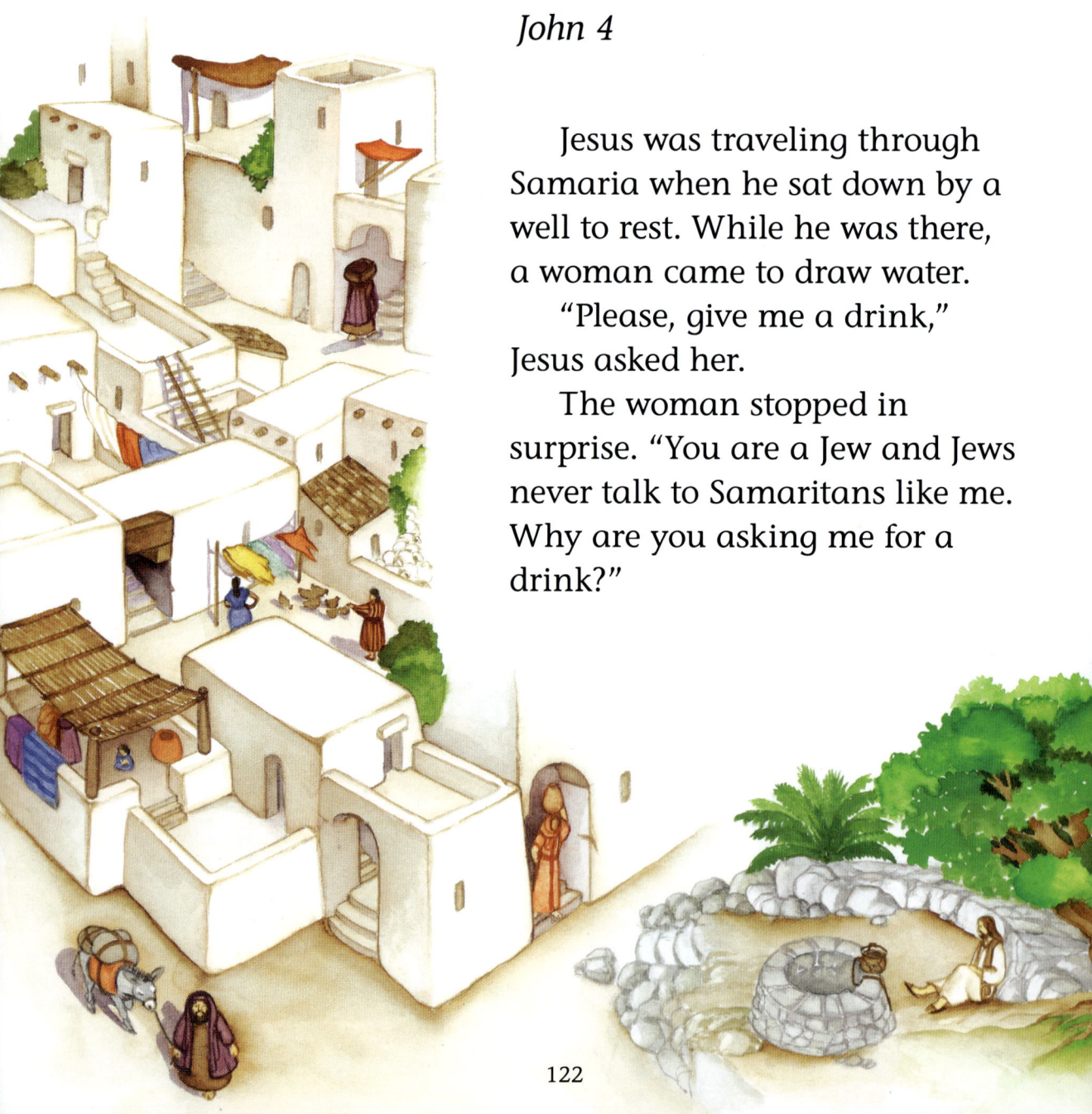

Jesus was traveling through Samaria when he sat down by a well to rest. While he was there, a woman came to draw water.

"Please, give me a drink," Jesus asked her.

The woman stopped in surprise. "You are a Jew and Jews never talk to Samaritans like me. Why are you asking me for a drink?"

Jesus answered, "If you knew who I was, you would be asking me for a drink instead. And I would give you living water."

"How can you get this living water?" she asked. "You have no bucket!"

Jesus told her, "If you drink the water I will give, you will never thirst. You will have eternal life."

"Give me this water, so I do not have to use a well," the woman replied.

"Go call your husband, and return here with him," Jesus said.

"I don't have a husband," she answered.

Jesus said, "You are right. In fact, you have had five husbands, and you are not married to the man you live with now."

124

The woman was amazed that Jesus knew so much about her. "I see you are a man of God," she said. "I know the Savior is coming. When he does, he will tell us everything."

"I am he," Jesus said.

Then the woman ran back to her village and told her neighbors about Jesus. They returned to the well with her. They listened to Jesus' words and believed.

*Jesus, I believe you are the Savior of the world. When I am with you, I have everything I need.*

# The Sermon on the Mount

*Matthew 5–7*

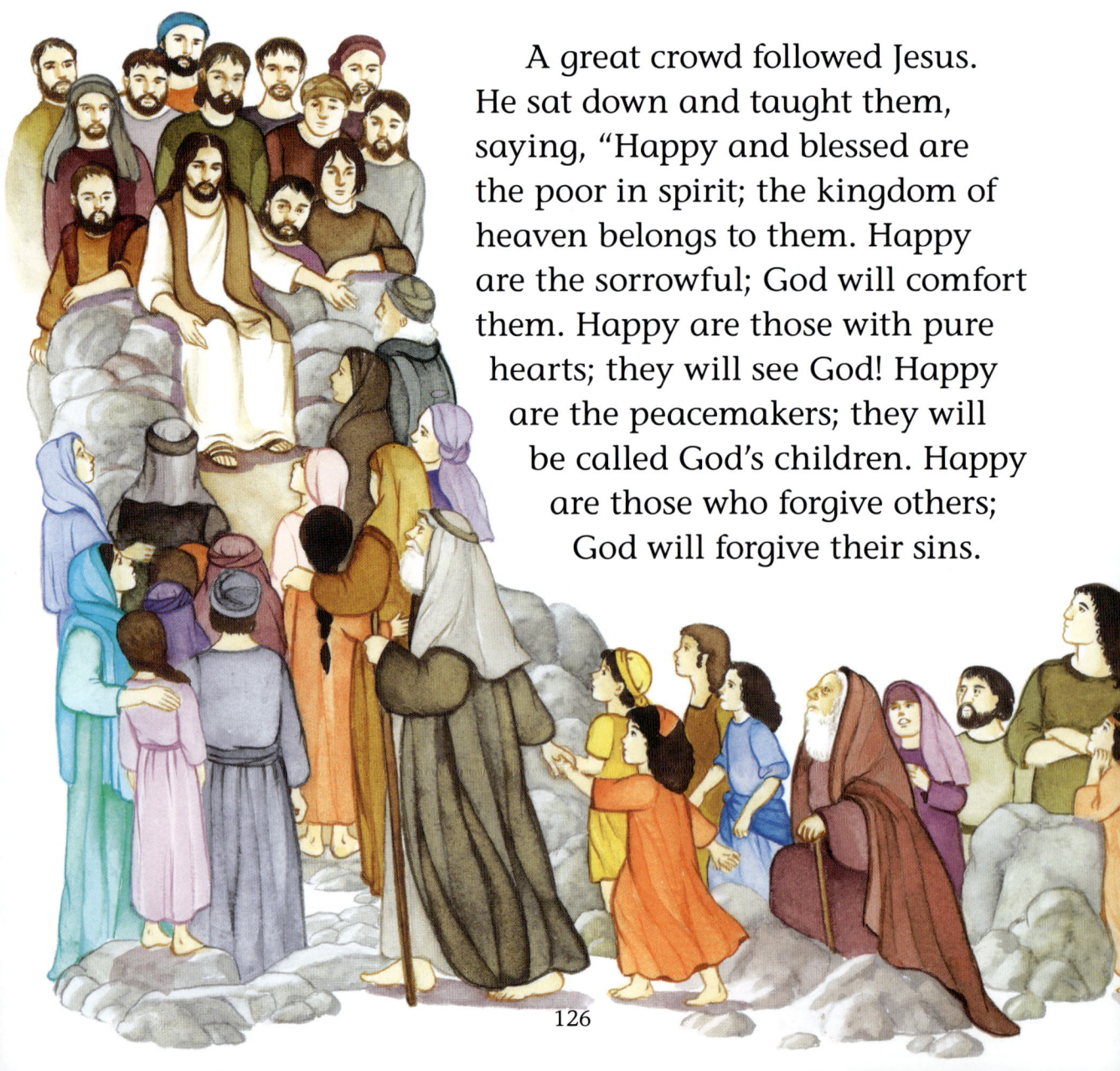

A great crowd followed Jesus. He sat down and taught them, saying, "Happy and blessed are the poor in spirit; the kingdom of heaven belongs to them. Happy are the sorrowful; God will comfort them. Happy are those with pure hearts; they will see God! Happy are the peacemakers; they will be called God's children. Happy are those who forgive others; God will forgive their sins.

Happy are you when people hurt or make fun of you because of me. You will have a great reward in heaven!"

Jesus continued, "You are the light of the world. Let your light shine by doing good things. Then people will see and bless your heavenly Father, who is working through you."

*Jesus, help me be a light for the world by doing good.*

# The Our Father

## *Matthew 6*

Jesus told his followers, "Love and pray for those who have hurt you. When you do this, you show that you are children of your heavenly Father.

"When you pray, you do not need many words. Your Father knows what you need. This is how you should pray: 'Our Father, who art in Heaven, hallowed be thy name. Thy kingdom come, thy will be done on earth as it is in heaven. Give us this day our daily bread, and forgive us our trespasses, as we forgive those who trespass against us. And lead us not into temptation, but deliver us from evil. Amen.'"

*Father, help me love and pray for every person. Help the world know that we are all your children.*

# The Daughter of Jairus

*Mark 5*

Jesus was speaking to a large crowd. Suddenly, a man named Jairus came and knelt before him. "My daughter is very sick. Please, come and cure her!" he begged. Jesus went with Jairus. The crowd followed and continued to surround him as he walked.

One of the women in the crowd had been sick for twelve years. She thought, "If I can just touch Jesus' cloak, I will be healed." She did so and was instantly cured.

Jesus sensed that God's power had gone out to someone. "Who touched me?" he asked.

"Everyone is crowding around and touching you!" his disciples answered.

But the woman knew Jesus was looking for her. She fearfully stepped forward and told him everything.

Jesus looked kindly at her and said, "Your faith has saved you. Go in peace and be healed."

While he was speaking, some people came with a message for Jairus. "Your daughter is dead," they reported. "Do not bother the teacher anymore."

Jesus overheard this and said to Jairus, "Do not be afraid. Just believe."

When they reached the house, Jesus took Peter, James, and John inside with him. The girl's family was weeping loudly. "Why are you crying?" Jesus asked them. "She is not

dead; only sleeping." Jesus sent everyone outside except his disciples and the girl's parents. He approached the girl, took her hand, and said, "Rise, little girl!" Immediately she opened her eyes, got up, and walked around. Jesus turned to her parents and said, "Give her something to eat." Everyone was amazed.

*Jesus, help me remember that I never have to be afraid because you are always with me.*

# The Multiplication of the Loaves and Fishes

*John 6*

Jesus saw a large crowd coming toward him and his disciples. Jesus asked Philip, "Where can we buy food for everyone?"

"We could never afford to feed so many!" Philip answered.

Andrew, another disciple, added, "Here is a boy with five loaves of bread and two fish. But what good is this for five thousand people?"

Jesus said, "Have everyone sit down." He took the bread and fish in his hands, thanked God for the food, and passed them around for the people to eat. When all had eaten, Jesus told his disciples, "Collect the leftovers so nothing will be wasted." They filled twelve baskets with leftovers.

The people saw this and said, "This must be the prophet God promised us!" They wanted to make Jesus king.

When Jesus found out, he quickly left them.

*Jesus, I offer you all I have. Help me to serve you and others with the gifts you have given me.*

# Jesus Walks on the Water

*Matthew 14*

Jesus told his disciples to cross the sea to the next town. After they left, he spent hours alone in prayer with his Father.

Early the next morning, Jesus caught up with his disciples by walking across the water toward their boat.

When the disciples saw him, they were terrified. But Jesus called out to them, "It is I! Do not be afraid."

Peter replied, "Lord, if it is you, tell me to join you on the water."

"Come," Jesus said.

Peter stepped out of the boat and began to walk on the water. But when he felt the strong wind, he panicked and began to sink. "Lord, help me!" he cried.

Jesus caught him at once. "Why did you doubt?" he asked Peter. They both returned to the boat, and the wind stopped.

*Jesus, help me to keep my eyes on you and to believe you will always be there to catch me when I ask for your help.*

# The Bread of Life

*John 6*

Many people followed Jesus after the miracle of the loaves and fish. Jesus said to them, "You are following me because I gave you food. Do not work for food that runs out, but for the food that lasts forever."

"How can we do the works of God?" they asked.

"This is the work of God: that you believe in me," Jesus said.

"What can you do to help us believe?" the people asked. "Moses gave our ancestors bread from heaven. What will you do?"

Jesus answered, "That bread did not come from Moses. It came from my Father. My Father's bread gives life to the world."

"Give us this bread always!" they exclaimed.

Jesus answered, "I am the Bread of Life from heaven. Whoever comes to me will never hunger. Whoever believes in me will never thirst."

The people did not understand. "How can this man say he comes from heaven?" they wondered.

Jesus replied, "No one can come to me unless the Father leads him. But I will give eternal life to everyone who comes. I am the Bread of Life. Whoever eats my Body and drinks my Blood remains in me forever, and I remain in him."

The crowd struggled with these words. "Who can do this?" they asked. Many who could not understand what Jesus was saying began to leave.

Then Jesus turned to his twelve disciples. "Do you want to leave, too?" he asked.

Simon Peter answered, "Lord, who else can we follow? You are the one God sent."

*Lord, thank you for giving yourself to me in the Eucharist! Help me receive you with love and remain with you forever.*

142

# Who Do You Say That I Am?

## Matthew 16

One day, Jesus asked his disciples, "What do people say about me?"

They answered, "Some say you are John the Baptist. Others think you are one of the prophets."

"Who do you say that I am?" Jesus asked.

Peter said, "You are the Christ, the Son of the living God."

"Blessed are you, Simon!" Jesus replied. "It was my Father in heaven who revealed this to you. Now you are Peter. You are the rock upon which I will build my Church and the powers of death will never overcome it."

*Lord Jesus, bless our Pope, the successor of Saint Peter. Help him guide everyone into the one Church you built for us.*

# Who Is Jesus?
# The Father Answers

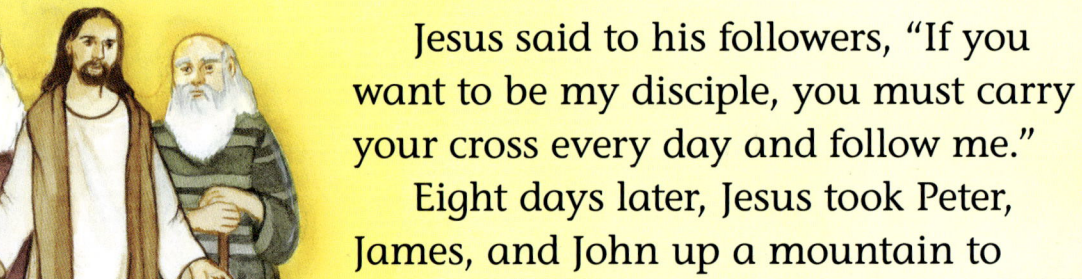

*Luke 9*

Jesus said to his followers, "If you want to be my disciple, you must carry your cross every day and follow me."

Eight days later, Jesus took Peter, James, and John up a mountain to pray. The disciples were very tired, but worked hard to stay awake while Jesus spoke with his Father.

Suddenly, Jesus' clothing turned white as light. Moses and Elijah appeared beside him. They began speaking to Jesus about the suffering he would go through on the cross.

The three disciples were wide awake now and terribly frightened. Finally, Peter spoke up. "Master, it is good that we are here!" he said. "Let us make three tents: one for you, one for Moses, and one for Elijah." But Peter was too amazed to know what he was saying.

At that moment, a cloud covered the disciples and a voice spoke. "This is my beloved Son. Listen to him!" Then the cloud was gone and the disciples were alone with Jesus.

Peter, James, and John followed Jesus down the mountain. They did not tell anyone what they had seen.

*Jesus, help me "carry my cross" and follow you. Teach me to love and serve others, especially when it feels hard to do.*

# A Good Neighbor

*Luke 10*

Jesus often used stories to teach people about the kingdom of God. One day, someone asked him, "Teacher, how can I live forever?"

Jesus answered, "What does God's law say?"

The man replied, "Love God with all your heart, mind, and strength, and love your neighbor as yourself."

Jesus said, "You are right. Do this and you will live."

"But who is my neighbor?" the man asked.

Jesus answered with a story. "Once, a man was attacked by robbers on the road. The robbers beat him and took everything he had and left him on the side of the road. He was badly hurt and could not move.

"Some time later, a priest passed by. He saw the man but did not stop to help him. Then a Levite came. He also saw the man, but he crossed to the other side of the road and kept walking.

Finally, a Samaritan came by. When he saw the injured man, his heart went out to him and he stopped to help. He cleaned and bandaged the man's wounds and took him to an inn, where he stayed and cared for him overnight.

"The next day, the Samaritan gave the innkeeper some money. 'I have to continue my journey,' he told the innkeeper. 'Please take care of this man for me. If you spend more money than what I have given you, I will repay you on my way back.'

"Now," said Jesus, "who was a neighbor to the robbers' victim?"

The man replied, "The one who cared for him."

Jesus said, "Go and do the same."

*Jesus, help me pay attention to the needs of others and do all I can to help them.*

# The Prodigal Son

*Luke 15*

Some people saw Jesus spending time with sinners. "How can you be around people who disobey God?" they asked. Jesus answered them with a story about God's mercy.

"Once, there was a father with two sons. One day, the younger son said to his father, 'Give me the money I will inherit from you after you die.'

When his father had done so, the son packed his things and traveled far away. He wasted his inheritance on fancy things and parties.

"Then famine struck, and the son began to starve. He took a job on a farm, but he still had nothing to eat. Finally, he thought to himself, 'My father's servants have plenty of food. I will go home and ask my father to treat me like one of his servants. I do not deserve to be called his son after what I have done.'

"The son began his journey home. When he was still far off, his father saw him coming and ran to meet him. The son started to apologize, saying, 'Father, I have sinned. I do not deserve to be called your son.'

"But the father called his servants and said, 'Quick! Find a robe, a ring, and sandals for my son to wear. Prepare the best food in the house. We must celebrate! My son was dead, but now he is alive!' The party began at once.

"Meanwhile, the older son was working in the fields. When he returned home, he heard music and asked a servant what was going on.

"'Your brother is home, and your father is celebrating his safe return!' the servant replied. On hearing this, the older son refused to enter the house. His father came out and

begged him to come inside, but the son replied, 'I have worked hard for you all my life, and you have never thrown a party for me! But now you hold a feast for the son who wasted your money?'

"The father answered, 'Son, you are always with me. Everything I have is yours. But now we must celebrate. Your brother was dead, but is alive again. He was lost and has been found.'"

*Lord, you never get tired of forgiving us, just like the father in your story. Thank you for your love!*

155

# Jesus Blesses the Children

*Luke 18*

Parents were bringing their babies and children to Jesus so he could lay his hands on them and bless them. When Jesus' disciples saw this, they told them to go away. But Jesus called the children to come closer. "Let the little children come to me. Do not stop them," he said to his disciples. "The kingdom of God belongs to little ones like these. Whoever wants to enter the kingdom of God must receive it like a child."

*Thank you, Jesus, for calling me close to you. Help me love you even more as I grow older!*

# The Raising of Lazarus

*John 11*

As Jesus traveled with his disciples, he got a message from his friends Mary and Martha in Bethany. "Our brother, Lazarus, is very sick," the messenger told him.

When Jesus heard this news he told his disciples, "This sickness will not end in death. It will reveal God's glory." They stayed where they were for two more days.

When Jesus and his followers arrived in Bethany, they received news that Lazarus had died. Martha ran to meet Jesus and said, "Lord, if you had been here, Lazarus would not have died."

"Your brother will rise again," Jesus told her. "I am the Resurrection and the Life. Whoever believes in me will not die. Do you believe this?"

"Yes, Lord," Martha replied. "I believe you are the Son of God."

Martha returned home and found her sister, Mary. "Jesus is asking for you," Martha told her.

Mary got up and went to Jesus in tears, followed by her family and friends. When Jesus saw their grief, his heart went out to them. He cried too.

"Where is Lazarus buried?" Jesus asked.

They took him to a large cave with a big stone in front of it.

"Remove the stone," Jesus said. Then he looked toward heaven and prayed. "Father, thank you for hearing my prayer. I know you always hear me. Help everyone believe that you sent me." Then he shouted, "Lazarus, come out!"

Lazarus came out of the tomb at once. He was alive!

From that day, many began to believe in Jesus.

In a different place, the Pharisees were talking about Jesus. They feared the Romans would punish their people because of Jesus, so they wanted him dead. The chief priest, Caiaphas, said, "Is it not better for one man to die instead of our whole nation?"

*Jesus, I believe you give us everlasting life. Thank you for creating me to be with you forever!*

# Entrance into Jerusalem

*Matthew 21; Mark 11; Luke 19; and John 12*

It was almost Passover, and Jesus and his disciples were making their way toward Jerusalem for the feast. When they reached the outskirts of the city, Jesus stopped. He called two of his disciples and said, "Go into the village. You will find a donkey there that has never been

ridden. Bring it here. If anyone questions you, tell them, 'The Lord needs it.'"

The disciples obeyed. When they returned with the donkey, Jesus mounted it and rode into the city of Jerusalem. The Scripture passage had finally come true, which read, "Jerusalem, here comes your king, meek and riding on a donkey." Jesus wanted to give the people this sign that he was the Messiah sent by God.

Great crowds came to see Jesus and honor him for his miracles. They used their cloaks and cut palm leaves to carpet the street in front of him. They waved branches as he passed and shouted, "Hosanna, Son of David! Blessed is he who comes in God's name!" The entire city heard the noise.

"Who is this man?" the people asked.

"This is the prophet Jesus from Nazareth!" the crowd replied.

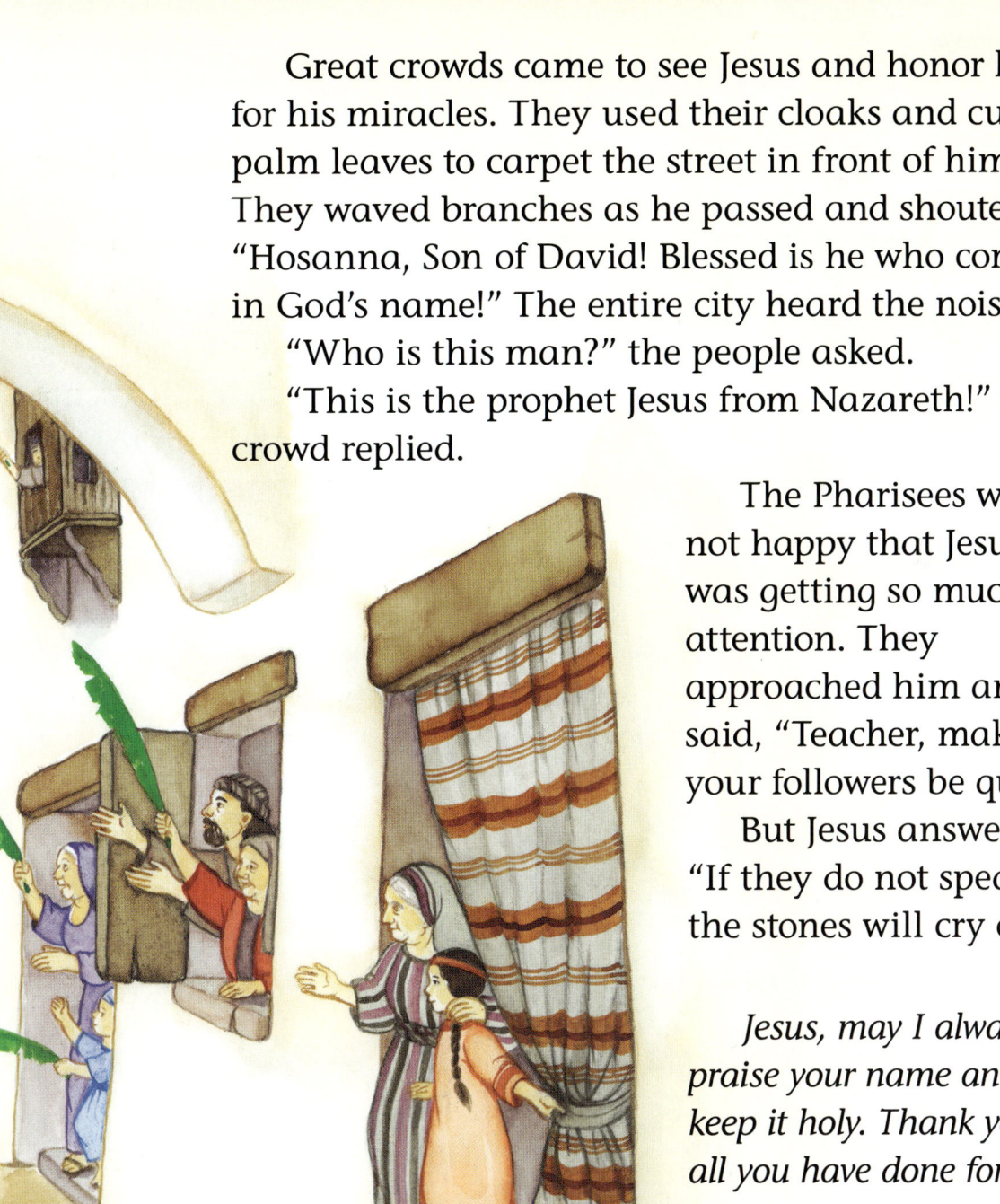

The Pharisees were not happy that Jesus was getting so much attention. They approached him and said, "Teacher, make your followers be quiet!"

But Jesus answered, "If they do not speak, the stones will cry out!"

*Jesus, may I always praise your name and keep it holy. Thank you for all you have done for me!*

# The Last Supper

*Luke 22*

The feast of Passover had arrived. Jesus found a large, upper room in someone's home where he could celebrate with his disciples. He sent Peter and John ahead of him to prepare the Passover meal.

When all were at table, Jesus said to his disciples, "I have been longing to eat this meal with you before I suffer." He took a loaf of bread in his hands, thanked God for it, broke it, and passed it around to them. "This is my Body, which I am giving up for you," Jesus said. "Do this in memory of me." When everyone had eaten, he took a cup filled with wine. He gave thanks to God and passed the cup around to them, saying, "This is my Blood. It will be poured out for you."

Then Jesus continued. "Someone will betray me. He is here with me at this table." The disciples began to ask one another, "Which one of us could it be? Who would do such a thing?"

A little while later they argued about who should be considered Jesus' greatest disciple.

Jesus said to them, "The greatest among you must be like the youngest. The leader must be like the servant. Learn from me. I am with you as the one who serves."

*Jesus, you invite me to this Supper at every Mass. Thank you for giving me your Body and Blood in Holy Communion. Help me to believe this is truly you!*

# Peter's Denial Foretold

*Luke 22*

Jesus looked at his disciples after they finished supper. He said to them, "You have always stayed by me, even when times were hard. One day, you will eat and drink with me in my kingdom."

Then Jesus turned to Peter and said, "Simon, listen to me. Satan wants you to follow him, but I have prayed for you to hold onto your faith. After you are tested, you must help your brothers."

Peter replied, "Lord, I am ready to go to prison and die with you!"

Jesus answered, "Before the rooster crows tomorrow morning, you will deny that you know me three times."

*Lord, help me believe and follow you, even when it is hard.*

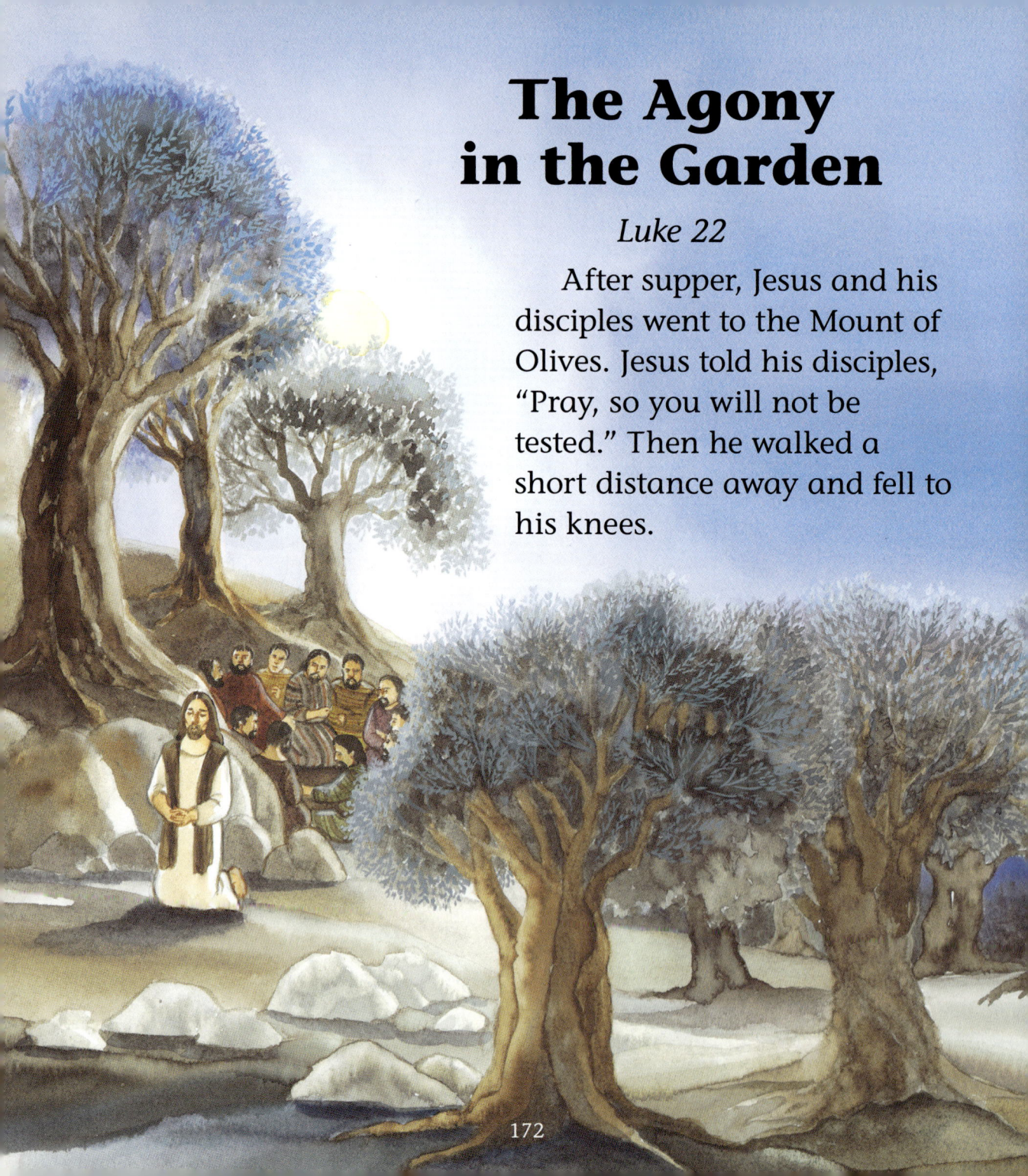

# The Agony
# in the Garden

*Luke 22*

After supper, Jesus and his disciples went to the Mount of Olives. Jesus told his disciples, "Pray, so you will not be tested." Then he walked a short distance away and fell to his knees.

"Father," Jesus prayed, "take this trial and let this cup pass away from me. But let your will be done; not mine." He was in such agony, he began to sweat blood.

When he finished his prayer, a crowd approached with swords and clubs. Judas was leading them. When Judas saw Jesus, he walked up to him and kissed him. Jesus said, "Judas, are you betraying me with a kiss?" Immediately, the crowd arrested Jesus and took him to the high priest.

Peter followed them until he reached the high priest's courtyard. There, he joined a group of people warming themselves by a fire. One of them saw Peter and said, "This man was with Jesus."

"I don't know Jesus," Peter replied.

A moment later, someone else saw him and said, "You are one of Jesus' followers."

"No, I'm not!" Peter said.

An hour later, someone else spoke up. "Surely, this man was with Jesus!"

"I don't know what you're talking about!" Peter shouted.

At that moment, a rooster crowed. Jesus heard the sound from inside the high priest's house and turned to look at Peter. Their eyes met. Then Peter remembered what Jesus had said: "Before the rooster crows, you will deny me three times." Peter left the courtyard in tears.

*Jesus, give me the courage to say that I believe in you and love you.*

# Before Pilate

*Matthew 27, Mark 15, Luke 23, John 18*

The chief priests brought Jesus to Pontius Pilate, the Roman governor, for questioning.

Pilate asked Jesus, "Are you the King of the Jews?"

"My kingdom does not belong to this world," Jesus replied.

Pilate asked him a few more questions. Then he returned to the chief priests and the growing crowd. "This man is not guilty of anything," he said. Still, he hoped to satisfy the chief priests, so he had Jesus beaten. Later he said, "It is the Passover. You have a tradition of asking me to release one prisoner for you every Passover. Should I release Jesus?"

"Not Jesus. Barabbas!" they answered. Barabbas was a murderer.

"Then what should I do with Jesus?" Pilate asked.

"Crucify him!" the crowd shouted.

So Pilate handed Jesus over to be crucified.

*Lord Jesus, help me stand up for people who are treated unfairly.*

# The Crucifixion

*Luke 23, John 19*

Pilate's soldiers took Jesus away to be crucified. They dressed him in a purple cloak and pressed a crown of thorns onto his head. They mocked him, saying, "Hail, King of the Jews!" Then they forced him to carry a heavy cross to Calvary, where he would be crucified.

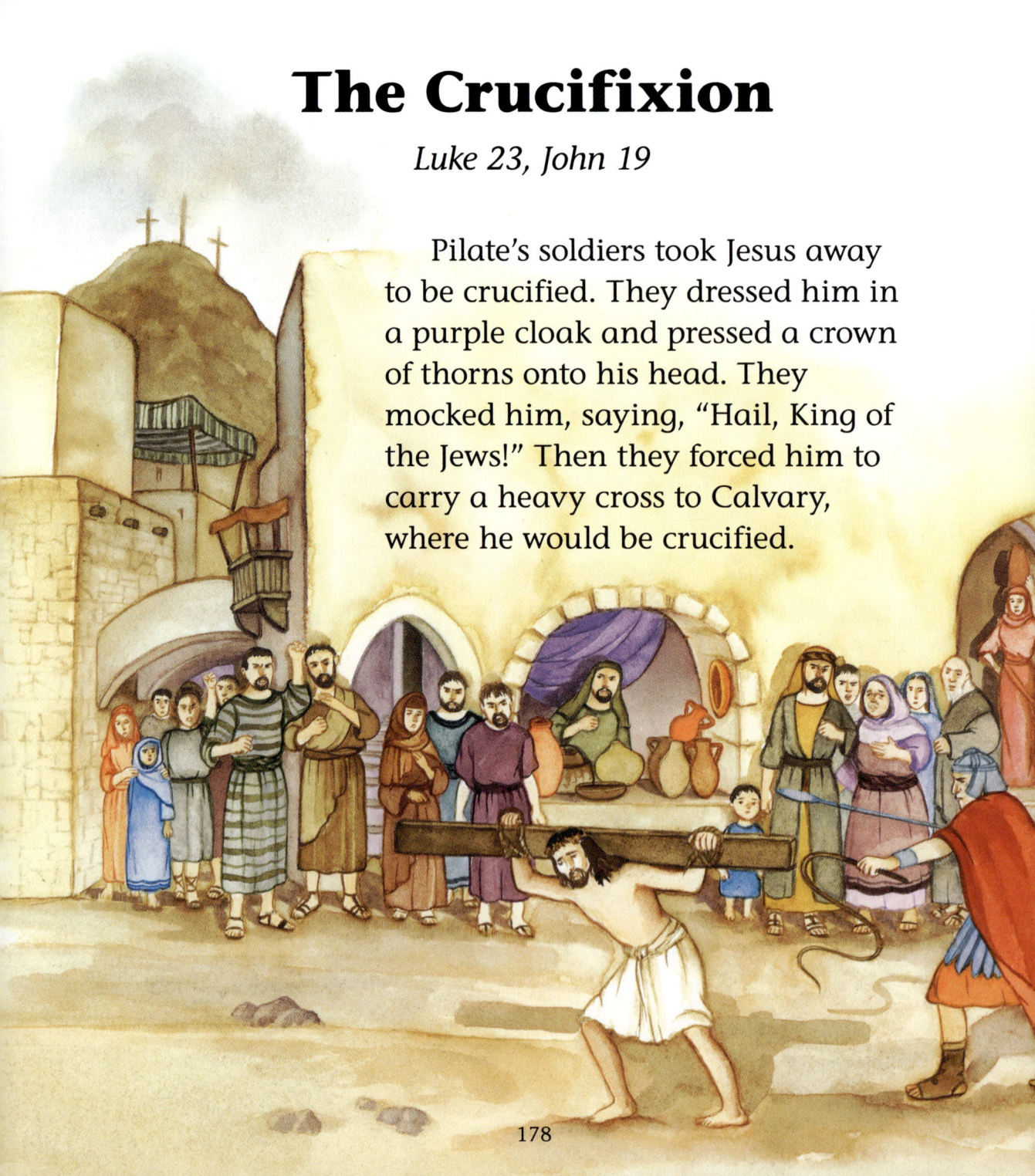

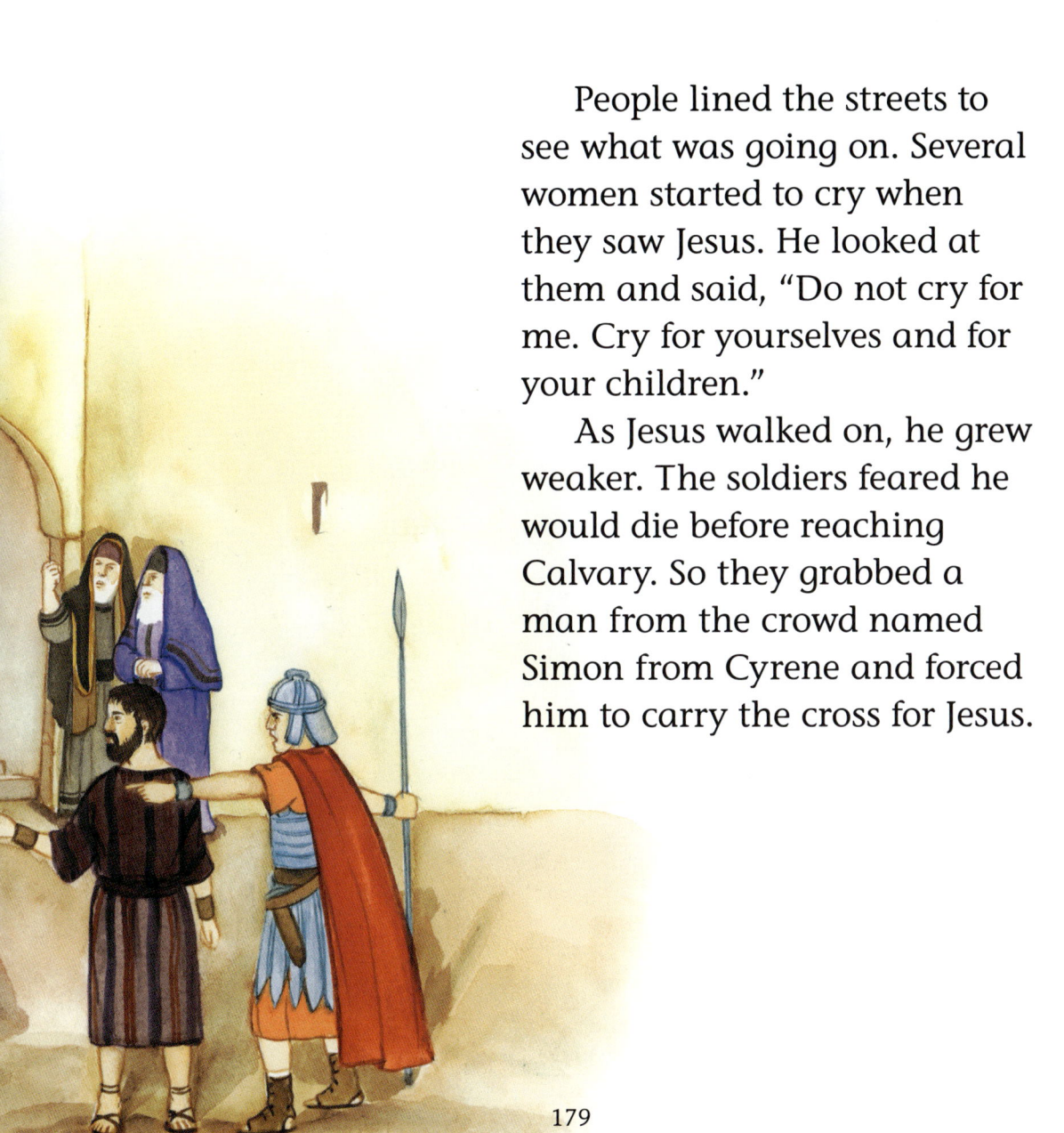

People lined the streets to see what was going on. Several women started to cry when they saw Jesus. He looked at them and said, "Do not cry for me. Cry for yourselves and for your children."

As Jesus walked on, he grew weaker. The soldiers feared he would die before reaching Calvary. So they grabbed a man from the crowd named Simon from Cyrene and forced him to carry the cross for Jesus.

When they got to Calvary, the soldiers nailed Jesus to the cross between two thieves. The thief on his left made fun of him. "If you are the Son of God, save yourself and us!" he shouted.

But the other thief defended Jesus. "This man has done nothing wrong," he said. Then he turned to Jesus and said, "Remember me when you come into your kingdom."

Jesus answered, "Today, you will be with me in paradise."

After three hours on the cross, Jesus took his final breaths. "Father, forgive these people. They do not know what they are doing," he prayed aloud. Then he looked up to heaven. "It is finished," he said. "Father, into your hands I commend my spirit." And with these words, Jesus died and handed himself over to his Father.

*Jesus, you forgave those who crucified you. Help me forgive those who hurt me.*

181

# The Resurrection

*John 20*

The soldiers took Jesus' body down from the cross. Joseph of Arimathea, a follower of Jesus, took the body and wrapped it in burial cloths. He laid it in a new cave and rolled a large stone over the entrance. Jesus' friends went home that night with heavy hearts.

Mary Magdalene returned to the tomb early on Sunday morning. She found the tomb open, and she ran to tell the disciples. Peter and another disciple immediately raced to the tomb and went inside. Jesus' body was gone. All they could find were the burial cloths.

After the disciples left, Mary returned to the tomb in tears. Where could Jesus' body be? But when she looked in the tomb, she saw two angels sitting there.

"Why are you crying?" the angels asked.

Mary answered, "Someone has taken my Lord!"

She turned around and saw a man standing behind her. "Woman, why are you crying?" he asked.

Mary responded, "Sir, if you took Jesus away, tell me where he is and I will take him."

"Mary!" the man replied.

Suddenly, Mary recognized him. It was Jesus!

Jesus said to her, "Go, tell my brothers, 'I am going to my Father and your Father, to my God and your God.'"

Mary ran back to the disciples. "I have seen the Lord! He is alive!" she said.

She told them everything Jesus said to her.

*Jesus, I believe you rose from the dead!*

# Thomas

*John 20*

On the evening of the Resurrection, the disciples gathered together and locked the doors of the house where they were staying. They were afraid the people who had killed Jesus might come after them, too. Suddenly, Jesus appeared in the room with them. "Peace be with you," he said. Then he showed them his wounded hands and his side. The disciples were overjoyed to see the Lord!

"Peace be with you," Jesus repeated. "The Father has sent me. Now, I send you." He breathed on them and said, "Receive the Holy Spirit. If you forgive others, their sins will be forgiven." Then Jesus left.

Now Thomas, one of the disciples, was not there when Jesus appeared. When he returned to the house, the disciples excitedly shared the news. "We have seen Jesus!" they exclaimed.

Thomas replied, "I will not believe unless I see and touch his wounds myself."

One week later, all the disciples, including Thomas, were gathered in the house. The doors were still locked, but once again Jesus came and stood with them. "Peace be with you," he said. Then Jesus said to Thomas, "See the wounds in my hands and side, and put your finger here. Do not doubt. Believe!"

Thomas cried out, "My Lord and my God!"
Jesus said, "Do you believe because you have seen me? Blessed are those who have not seen me, but still believe."

*Lord, I have not seen you, but I believe in you. Thank you for giving me the gift of faith.*

# The Road to Emmaus

*Luke 24*

After Jesus rose from the dead, two of his followers left Jerusalem to go to Emmaus. They discussed the events of the last few days as they walked. Then Jesus approached and began to walk with them, but he made it so they did not recognize him. "What are you talking about?" Jesus asked.

One of them, named Cleopas, answered, "Are you the only visitor to Jerusalem who does not know what happened there?"

"What do you mean?" Jesus asked.

They replied, "Everything that happened to Jesus. We thought he was the Messiah, but our leaders crucified him three days ago. Then this morning, some women from our group went to his tomb. They came back and told us Jesus is alive!"

Jesus said, "You are so slow to believe! Didn't the prophets say the Messiah would suffer before entering into his glory?" Then he explained all the Scriptures that spoke about his Passion, death, and Resurrection.

When they reached Emmaus, the disciples invited the stranger to stay with them. Jesus agreed and joined them for supper. He took bread, blessed it, broke it, and gave it to them. Suddenly, the disciples recognized him. They knew this was Jesus! But then Jesus vanished from sight. The disciples turned to one another and said, "Weren't our hearts on fire as he spoke about the Scriptures?" They immediately returned to Jerusalem to tell the disciples what happened.

*Jesus, help me recognize you at Mass, in your word and in the Eucharist.*

# Jesus and Peter

*John 21*

Jesus appeared to his disciples again by the Sea of Tiberius.

Several of the disciples were gathered at the seashore when Peter told them, "I am going fishing."

"We will go with you," the disciples replied.

They boarded their boat and fished all night, but they did not catch anything.

At daybreak, a man from the shore called out to them. "Children, have you caught any fish yet?" he asked.

"No," they shouted back.

"Throw your nets to the right side of the boat," the man suggested. "You will find fish there."

The disciples obeyed. They caught so many fish that they could not pull their nets back into the boat!

One of the disciples said to Peter, "It is the Lord."

When Peter heard this, he jumped into the sea and swam to shore. The disciples followed in the boat with their catch of fish.

When they reached shore, they saw Jesus cooking fish over a campfire. "Bring some of the fish you just caught," he said to them, "and come have breakfast." Then Jesus took the fish and some bread he had brought and gave it to them.

When they had eaten, Jesus asked Peter three times, "Simon, son of John, do you love me?"

"Yes, Lord, you know that I love you," Peter answered. He wondered why Jesus asked him three times if he loved him.

"Then feed my lambs. Care for my sheep. And follow me," Jesus replied.

*Lord, give wisdom, courage, and holiness to your bishops. Thank you for calling them to be shepherds of your Church.*

# Jesus Ascends to Heaven

*Acts 1*

Jesus appeared to his disciples many times after his Resurrection and spoke to them about the kingdom of God. Forty days after his Resurrection, Jesus knew it was time to return to his Father in heaven. He called his disciples around him and said, "You will receive power from the Holy Spirit.

He will come upon you and make you my witnesses to the whole world." The disciples watched as Jesus ascended into heaven. Then a cloud passed in front of him. The disciples continued staring at the sky, but they could not see Jesus.

Suddenly, two men in white robes stood by them. "Why are you looking up at the sky?" the men asked. "Jesus will return in the same way you saw him go to heaven."

*Jesus, help me witness to you in all that I do today.*

# Pentecost

*Acts 2*

After Jesus ascended into heaven, the Apostles gathered in one place. They prayed constantly. Mary, the mother of Jesus, and many other disciples, men and women, prayed with them.

On the Jewish feast of Pentecost,
a sound like a strong wind
suddenly filled the house where
they were praying. Then
something like flames of fire
appeared and rested on each one
of them. They were filled with
the Holy Spirit and began to
speak in different
languages.

The people of Jerusalem heard about this and came to see the disciples. Despite coming from places all around the world, they understood all that the disciples said about God.

"What does this mean? How can I hear them in my native language?" each one of them wondered.

Peter stood up and addressed them. "Friends, God promised to send us his Spirit through the prophets. Now the Spirit has given us power to tell you about Jesus of Nazareth. Jesus was sent

by God. You saw the miracles he worked. You killed him, but God raised him from the dead and made him Lord and Messiah. Repent and be baptized in his name. Then you too will receive the Holy Spirit, and all your sins will be forgiven."

Many people believed after listening to Peter. The disciples baptized about 3,000 people that day.

*Come, Holy Spirit! Fill me with the fire of your love!*

# The Conversion of Paul

*Acts 8–9*

As the disciples preached, more people began to believe in Jesus. The Jewish leaders did not like this and began to arrest the followers of Christ. One of these leaders was Saul of Tarsus.

Saul got permission from the high priest in Jerusalem to travel to Damascus and arrest any followers of Jesus he found along the way.

While Saul was walking toward the city, a bright light flashed around him. He fell to the ground, blinded from the light. Then he heard a voice say, "Saul, Saul! Why are you persecuting me?"

"Who are you, sir?" Saul asked.

The voice answered, "I am Jesus, the one you are attacking. When you hurt my followers, you hurt me. Now go into Damascus. You will be told what to do there."

Saul got up. The people who were
traveling with Saul were stunned and did
not know what to say. They had heard the
voice but had not seen anything. So they
took Saul, who was still blind, by the hand
and led him to Damascus.

Three days later, the Lord spoke to a
disciple in Damascus named Ananias.
"There is a man from Tarsus named Saul
staying in Damascus," he told him. "Go to
him and heal his blindness, for I have

chosen him to speak my name to the whole world." Ananias went, laid his hands on Saul, and baptized him.

Saul's blindness left him, and he immediately began to speak about Jesus to all the people in the synagogues. He took the name Paul and traveled across the known world to share the good news of Christ.

*Jesus, help me share
my love for you with others.*

# Come, Lord Jesus!

*Revelation 22*

In the last book of the Bible, Jesus says, "I am coming soon. Happy are those who keep my word. I am the beginning and the end of all things. I will reward each person for the good that they have done. I will give life-giving water to everyone who wants it. Truly, I am coming soon!"

*Come, Lord Jesus! Help me to live always with hope.*

# Prayers

## The Sign of the Cross

In the name of the Father, and of the Son, and of the Holy Spirit. Amen.

## Apostles' Creed

I believe in God, the Father almighty, Creator of heaven and earth, and in Jesus Christ, his only Son, our Lord, who was conceived by the Holy Spirit, born of the Virgin Mary, suffered under Pontius Pilate, was crucified, died and was buried; he descended to the dead; on the third day he rose again; he ascended into heaven and is seated at the right hand of God the Father almighty; from there he shall come to judge the living and the dead. I believe in the Holy Spirit, the holy catholic Church, the communion of saints, the forgiveness of sins, the resurrection of the body, and life everlasting. Amen.

## Our Father

Our Father, who art in heaven, hallowed be thy name; thy kingdom come; thy will be done on earth as it is in heaven. Give us this day our daily bread; and forgive us our trespasses as we forgive those who trespass against us; and lead us not into temptation, but deliver us from evil. Amen.

## Hail Mary

Hail Mary, full of grace, the Lord is with thee. Blessed art thou among women, and blessed is the fruit of thy womb, Jesus. Holy Mary, Mother of God, pray for us sinners, now and at the hour of our death. Amen.

## Glory

Glory to the Father, and to the Son, and to the Holy Spirit, as it was in the beginning, is now, and ever shall be, world without end. Amen.

## Hail, Holy Queen

Hail, holy Queen, Mother of Mercy, our life, our sweetness, and our hope. To thee do we cry, poor banished children of Eve; to thee do we send up our sighs, mourning, and weeping in this valley of tears. Turn then, most gracious advocate, thine eyes of mercy toward us, and after this our exile, show unto us the blessed fruit of thy womb, Jesus. O clement, O Loving, O sweet Virgin Mary.

## Angel of God

Angel of God, my guardian dear, to whom God's love entrusts me here, ever this day be at my side, to light and guard, to rule and guide. Amen.

## Morning Prayer

I adore you, my God. I love you with all my heart. Thank you for having created me and made me a Christian. Thank you for having kept me safe this night. Today I want to please you, Lord. I want to be all yours. Keep me from sin, Jesus. Bless everyone in my family. Bless all my friends. Amen.

## Night Prayer

I adore you, my God. I love you with all my heart. Thank you for the good things you helped me to do today! *(Remember some of these good things.)* I am sorry for the wrong things I did today. I know that you forgive me. Take care of me while I sleep, Lord. Please bless me and all those I love. Amen.

# How to Pray the Rosary

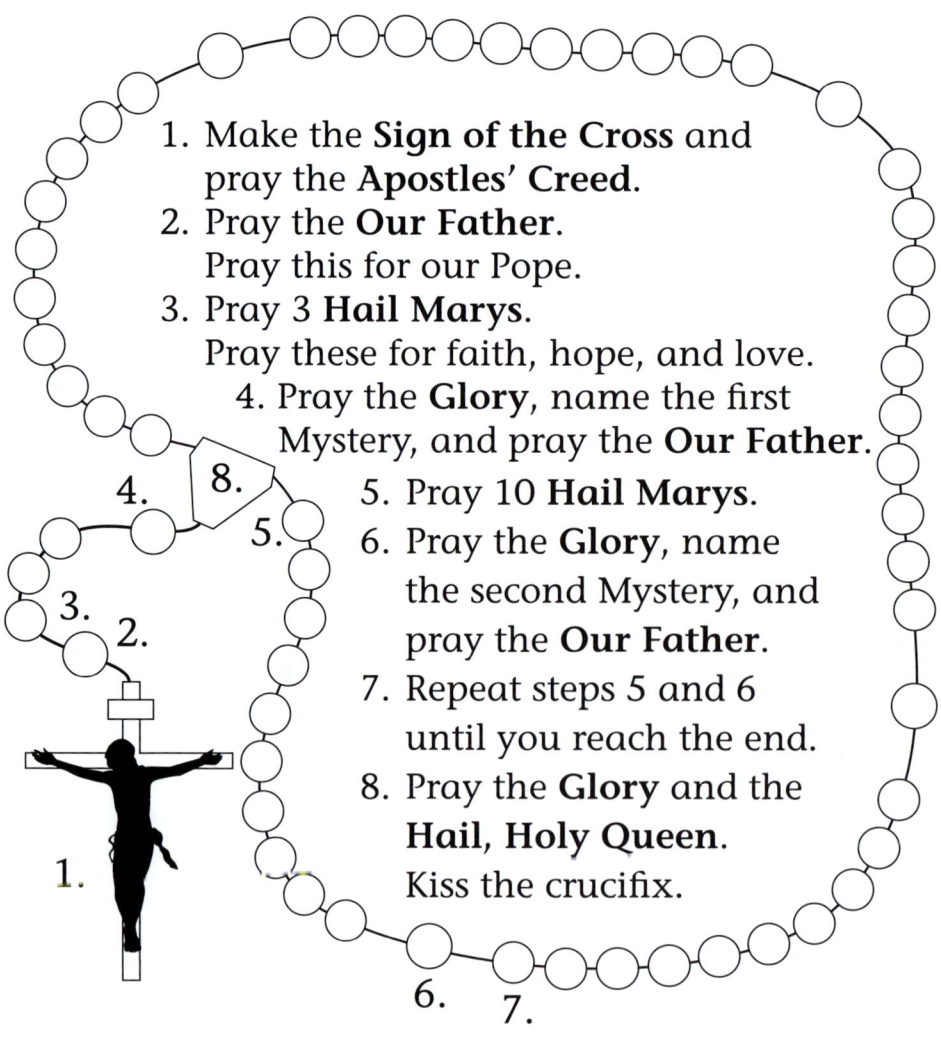

1. Make the **Sign of the Cross** and pray the **Apostles' Creed**.
2. Pray the **Our Father**.
   Pray this for our Pope.
3. Pray 3 **Hail Marys**.
   Pray these for faith, hope, and love.
4. Pray the **Glory**, name the first Mystery, and pray the **Our Father**.
5. Pray 10 **Hail Marys**.
6. Pray the **Glory**, name the second Mystery, and pray the **Our Father**.
7. Repeat steps 5 and 6 until you reach the end.
8. Pray the **Glory** and the **Hail, Holy Queen**.
   Kiss the crucifix.

# Mysteries

## Glorious Mysteries
### (Sundays and Wednesdays)

1. The Resurrection of Jesus (p. 182)
2. The Ascension of Jesus into Heaven (p. 196)
3. The Descent of the Holy Spirit (p. 198)
4. The Assumption of Mary into Heaven*
5. The Coronation of Mary as Queen of Heaven*

## Joyful Mysteries
### (Mondays and Saturdays)

1. The Annunciation (p. 100)
2. The Visitation (p. 103)
3. The Nativity (or the Birth) of Jesus (p. 104)
4. The Presentation of Jesus in the Temple (p. 108)
5. The Finding of Jesus in the Temple (p. 110)

## Sorrowful Mysteries
### (Tuesdays and Fridays)

1. The Agony in the Garden (p. 172)
2. The Scourging at the Pillar (p. 176)
3. The Crowning with Thorns (p. 178)
4. The Carrying of the Cross (p. 178)
5. The Crucifixion and Death of Jesus (p. 178)

## Luminous Mysteries
### (Thursdays)

1. The Baptism in the Jordan (p. 112)
2. The Wedding Feast at Cana (p. 120)
3. The Proclamation of the Kingdom of Heaven (p. 126)
4. The Transfiguration (p. 196)
5. The Institution of the Eucharist (p. 166)

* Although these two mysteries are not found in Scripture, the Church recognizes the importance of Mary as the Mother of God. Being without sin herself, the Church believes she is already in Heaven, soul *and* body. Also, because Jesus is the King of Heaven, his mother is the Queen of Heaven.

Journey of Abram (Abraham) (about 1850 B.C.)

MAP LEGEND
Fetile Crescent

Caspian Sea

Persian Gulf

Ur

Babylon

Tigris River

Euphrates River

Haran

Damascus

CANAAN

Sichem

Hebron

Mediterranean Sea

Mount Sinai

Red Sea

Nile River

EGYPT

Mediterranean Sea

CANAAN

Jordan River

Jericho

Mount Nebo

Dead Sea

Hebron

MOAB

Rameses

Cades-Barnea

SINAI PENINSULA

MIDIAN

EGYPT

Mount Sinai

Nile River

Route of the Israelites to Canaan

Red Sea

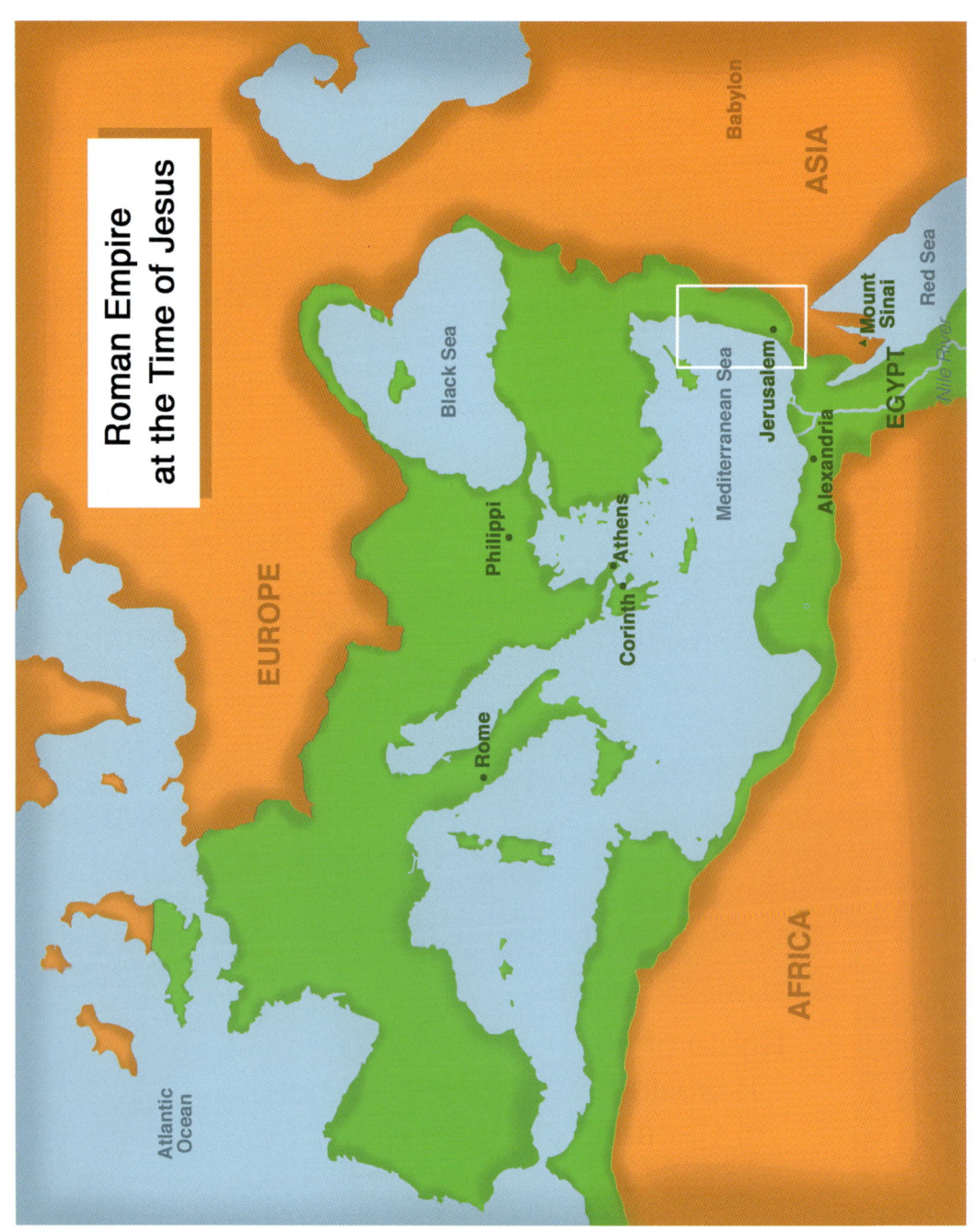

Roman Empire
at the Time of Jesus

EUROPE

ASIA

AFRICA

Atlantic
Ocean

Black Sea

Mediterranean Sea

Babylon

Red Sea

Mount
Sinai

Nile River

EGYPT

Alexandria

Jerusalem

Corinth

Athens

Philippi

Rome

Mount of the
Beatitudes

• Bethsaida

Capernaum •

GALILEE

Sea of
Galilee

• Cana

• Nazareth

Mount Tabor ▲

Mediterranean
Sea

SAMARIA

Jordan River

• Jerusalem

Emmaus •

• Bethlehem

JUDEA

• Hebron

Dead
Sea

**Israel at the
Time of Jesus**

215

# Who are the Daughters of St. Paul?

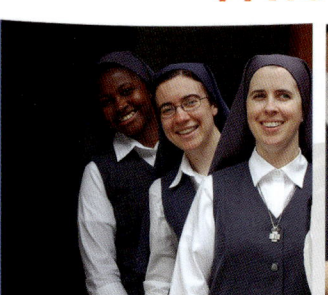   

We are Catholic sisters. Our mission is to be like Saint Paul and tell everyone about Jesus! There are so many ways for people to communicate with each other. We want to use all of them so everyone will know how much God loves us. We do this by printing books (you're holding one!), making radio shows, singing, helping people at our bookstores, using the internet, and in many other ways.

VISIT OUR WEB SITE AT WWW.PAULINE.ORG

**BOOKS & MEDIA**

The Daughters of St. Paul operate book and media centers at the following addresses. Visit, call, or write the one nearest you today, or find us at www.paulinestore.org.

**CALIFORNIA**
3908 Sepulveda Blvd, Culver City, CA 90230          310-397-8676
3250 Middlefield Road, Menlo Park, CA 94025         650-562-7060

**FLORIDA**
145 SW 107th Avenue, Miami, FL 33174                305-559-6715

**HAWAII**
1143 Bishop Street, Honolulu, HI 96813              808-521-2731

**ILLINOIS**
172 North Michigan Avenue, Chicago, IL 60601        312-346-4228

**LOUISIANA**
4403 Veterans Memorial Blvd, Metairie, LA 70006     504-887-7631

**MASSACHUSETTS**
885 Providence Hwy, Dedham, MA 02026                781-326-5385

**MISSOURI**
9804 Watson Road, St. Louis, MO 63126               314-965-3512

**NEW YORK**
115 E. 29th Street, New York City, NY 10016         212-754-1110

**SOUTH CAROLINA**
243 King Street, Charleston, SC 29401               843-577-0175

**TEXAS**
No book center; for parish exhibits or outreach evangelization, contact:
210-569-0500 or SanAntonio@paulinemedia.com or P.O. Box 761416, San
Antonio, TX 78245

**VIRGINIA**
1025 King Street, Alexandria, VA 22314              703-549-3806

**CANADA**
3022 Dufferin Street, Toronto, ON M6B 3T5           416-781-9131

# smile
## God loves you